IMAGES
of America

EARLY RENO

The date could be 1900, looking south on Virginia Street from the point where the Reno Arch will be built in 1926. The iron-arched bridge is at the end of the wide street, dating the picture to before 1905. To the right of the bridge is the first Riverside Hotel. Bicycles were an important means of transportation, with a few newfangled cars and some horse-drawn wagons and carriages parked on the street. Banners and American flags fly above the street, alternating with lines of electric lightbulbs—perhaps to celebrate Independence Day. (WA-2052.)

ON THE COVER: The first arch at Virginia Street and Commercial Row was erected in 1926 to celebrate the completion of the Lincoln and Victory Highways with Reno's 1927 Transcontinental Highways Exposition. Following the exposition, the Reno City Council decided to keep the arch and held a contest to name a slogan for Reno. The winning jingle, "The Biggest Little City in the World," was installed on the arch in 1929. Light bulbs illuminated the arch and the stylized torches that surround the city's name, making the nighttime view of the arch breathtaking. (WA-8004.)

IMAGES
of America
EARLY RENO

Nevada Historical Society
Docent Council

Copyright © 2011 by Nevada Historical Society Docent Council
ISBN 978-1-5316-5426-9

Published by Arcadia Publishing
Charleston, South Carolina

Library of Congress Control Number: 2010932070

For all general information, please contact Arcadia Publishing:
Telephone 843-853-2070
Fax 843-853-0044
E-mail sales@arcadiapublishing.com
For customer service and orders:
Toll-Free 1-888-313-2665

Visit us on the Internet at www.arcadiapublishing.com

This book is dedicated to the hardworking pioneers and settlers who believed in Reno and made it the "Biggest Little City in the World."

Contents

Foreword		6
Acknowledgments		7
Introduction		8
1.	Forming a Town The 1800s	11
2.	Becoming a City The Early 1900s	25
3.	Railroads Linking the Nation	47
4.	New Modes of Transportation Automobiles and Airplanes	57
5.	Surviving the Depression A Marriage and Divorce Destination	69
6.	Reno or Bust The Gaming Industry	77
7.	Institutions Schools, Hospitals, and the Historical Society	85
8.	Organizations Social, Fraternal, and Religious	97
9.	Coming of Age People, Occupations, and Businesses	105
10.	How Reno Plays Entertainment and Recreation	115
Bibliography		127

Foreword

Why work and publish another book on the history of early Reno? The 212 historical photographs and illustrations gathered from the Nevada Historical Society's collections will speak for themselves. Our *Early Reno* pictorial book is brimming with historical facts for history lovers of all ages.

The Nevada Historical Society (NHS), the state's oldest cultural institution, was formed on May 31, 1904. Without the foresight of Dr. Jeanne Elizabeth Wier, along with several members of the Nevada Academy of Sciences, the NHS might not have been created. The primary objective was to investigate topics pertaining to the history of Nevada and collect relics for a museum.

After 50 years of statehood, Wier was convinced that Nevada's pioneer stories and objects were vanishing. "We realize that the pioneers are rapidly passing away and that if this work is ever to be done in a satisfactory way, it must not be longer delayed," she said. Her passion in collecting historical materials spurred her to take many adventurous collecting trips.

Wier left her imprint on the first 50 years of the collections, as well as the scores of staff and volunteers throughout NHS's history. Our mission has not changed much in its original intent to collect, preserve, and educate the public on the history of the state of Nevada, the Great Basin, and the West. The collections housed at the Nevada Historical Society are truly amazing and will continue to be a valuable resource for future generations.

The process of watching the docent council put together this book underscores the importance of the council to the museum and the state of Nevada. NHS has been truly fortunate over the last 30 years in having these amazing volunteers who are crucial to fulfilling our mission. Our docents act as tour guides for our galleries, assist the public in our museum store and research library, and help work in the artifact, photograph, library, and manuscript collections—and, they produced this book.

We hope that you will enjoy this pictorial history and take away a newfound appreciation for Reno and the Nevada Historical Society.

—Sheryln L. Hayes-Zorn
Acting Director
Nevada Historical Society

Acknowledgments

The idea for the *Early Reno* book began with David Kennedy, president of the Nevada Historical Society Docent Council. David was initially contacted by Debbie Seracini, our Arcadia editor, to get the book project underway, and she worked with us throughout the project. David selected and scanned the photographs. Carol Coleman wrote the text and produced the layout. She was the pusher and detail person. Thanks to those who helped gather information and organize photographs.

Without the photograph archive of the Nevada Historical Society (NHS), this project would not have been possible. The NHS photography collection encompasses over 500,000 historical images, with more than 30,000 of the Reno area. Thanks to acting director Sheryln Hayes-Zorn for supporting us in this endeavor from the beginning. Lee Brumbaugh, the NHS curator of photography, patiently led us through the NHS's procedures for scanning and processing images. Without his expertise we could not have produced the book, and we thank him.

Several Reno historians have reviewed the book and we very much appreciate their support. Patty Cafferata, author of books about the Mapes, the Lake Mansion, and others; Neal Cobb and Jerry Fenwick, authors of *Reno, Now and Then*; and architectural historian Mella Rothwell Harmon—we owe a special thanks to all of you.

The information that Historic Reno Preservation Society's *FootPrints* quarterly provided to this book needs to be recognized, with thanks for their research and articles by authors Debbie Hinman, Kim Henrick, Mella Rothwell Harmon, Linda Sievers, Cindy Ainsworth, Sharon Walbridge, Lloyd Shanks, Patty Cafferata, Jon Wagner, Leanne Stone, John Marschall, Felvia Belaustegui, and Tim Mueller.

Nevada Historical Society Quarterlies were a wealth of information. Thanks to these authors for their research and articles: Mella Rothwell Harmon, Wendell Huffman, Ron James, Phil Earl, Peter Bandurraga, James Caron, Albin Cofone, Jeronima Echeverria, Jerome Edwards, Charles Jeffrey Garrison, Brian Scot Hagen, Jack Middleton, Larry Schweikart, Clifford Alpheus Shaw, James Stensvaag, Ralph Roske, and William Rowley.

All but six of the 212 images used in this book are from the archives of the Nevada Historical Society in Reno and have been provided here with their index number in the caption for the reader's convenience.

INTRODUCTION

Man has inhabited northern Nevada for 1,000 years or more. Small nomadic bands of Paiute, Shoshone, and Washo (not *Washoe*, the Americanized term) eked out an existence: the Paiute fishing at Pyramid Lake, the Washo moving to the western side of Lake Tahoe in summer and harvesting pine nuts near Carson City in the fall. These people were hunters, fishermen, and gatherers; they lived on what the land provided. They carried most of their possessions on their backs or travois from one camp to the next. It was a meager existence at best.

The first half of the 19th century was a time of extraordinary territorial growth for the United States. The Louisiana Purchase, completed in 1803, doubled the size of the country. The Lewis and Clark Expedition (1804–1806) was the first overland expedition to the West Coast undertaken by the government. The goal was to assess the resources being exchanged in the Louisiana Purchase and to lay the groundwork for westward expansion of the United States.

"Manifest Destiny" was a concept, first used by journalist John L. O'Sullivan, which influenced American policy in the 1800s. It was the driving force behind expansion into the west and was heavily promoted in the press. While it was not an official government policy, it led to the passage of the Homestead Act, which encouraged westward colonization.

Beginning in the 1840s, thousands of Americans headed to Oregon Country, the area west of the Rocky Mountains. Between 1842 and 1846, John Frémont and his guide Kit Carson led expedition parties on the Oregon Trail and into the Sierra Nevada. The discovery of gold in California in 1848 brought more than 100,000 people west, traveling over land on foot, by horse, and in covered wagons. There was a steady westward expansion of civilization, as people passed through Nevada on their way to California, seeking an improved life in mining or farming the rich soil. California was the destination—the vast majority of emigrants entering Nevada were on their way to other places.

Gold was discovered in Gold Canyon, near what is now Dayton, Nevada, in the spring of 1850, and miners made their way to the area. Silver was discovered on the Comstock Lode in 1859, and the town of Virginia City, Nevada, sprouted up almost overnight, with more than 800 buildings constructed by 1860. Before long, droves of miners, prospectors, merchants, and others were heading to Nevada to seek their fortunes. Many travelers heading for Virginia City crossed the bridge at Lake's Crossing, now the site of Reno's Virginia Street Bridge. Reno's Virginia Street was so named because it was one route to Virginia City, which rapidly became the largest and most important city in Nevada.

Abraham Lincoln, elected president in 1860, campaigned against the expansion of slavery beyond the states in which it already existed. In response, seven southern states seceded from the Union, and the Civil War over states' rights began in 1861. Congress approved the act to organize the Territory of Nevada, without slavery, in March 1861. An enabling act for Nevada statehood was signed by President Lincoln on March 21, 1864. The Civil War was being fought, and Nevada was perceived to be pro-Union and Republican. A Republican congressional delegation from Nevada could provide additional votes for the passage of the 13th Amendment to abolish slavery and support President Lincoln in the next election. Nevada submitted an approved state constitution to Congress in September 1864, and it was telegraphed to Washington, D.C., the longest and most expensive telegram ever sent up to that time. President Lincoln proclaimed Nevada the 36th state in the Union on October 31, 1864. Thus, the Civil War was responsible for rushing statehood to Nevada, one of the least populated of all the territories.

The idea for a transcontinental railroad to "shrink the continent and change the whole world," as described in Enid Johnson's book *Rails Across the Continent: The Story of the First Transcontinental Railroad*, was first proposed in 1832 by S. W. Dexter in *The Ann Arbor Emigrant*. In 1853, the Pacific Railroad Survey was authorized by Congress. In 1857, T. D. Judah, who designed the Central Pacific line, wrote "A Practical Plan for Building the Pacific Railroad." In 1862, Congress passed the Pacific Railway Act mandating that the Union Pacific Railway Company would build west from Omaha, Nebraska, and the Central Pacific Railroad Company east from Sacramento, California. It also provided for a telegraph line to be built adjacent to the railroad. The northern states had two main reasons to build the railroad: the first was to bind California to the Union so that it would not secede or be taken over by England, and the second was to ensure the shipment of troops, guns, and supplies to the west in a continuing war with the Native Americans.

After the seven southern states seceded from the Union, the votes were in place for Congress to authorize the northern route. The Civil War ended the debate over where to build the transcontinental railroad—no southern senators, no southern routes. The northern route for the first transcontinental railway was based on the economics of gold mining in California and the discovery of silver in Nevada's Comstock Lode.

The Railway Act of 1864 gave each railway company 20 square miles (12,800 acres) of public land for each mile of track built. The two railway companies were in competition for the land. The transcontinental railroad project began construction in 1863. In May 1868, the Central Pacific tracks reached the Truckee Meadows, where the railroad was to establish a depot; thus, the town of Reno was born. The town was named for Union general Jesse Reno, who died in 1862 in the Civil War battle of South Mountain. He never saw the town named for him. The Central Pacific Railroad met the Union Pacific Railroad at Promontory, Utah, in the spring of 1869.

The railroad was the primary form of transportation until highways and the automobile changed the lives of Reno residents and all Americans. With the automobile, people could travel in their own vehicles on their own schedules wherever they liked. During the first half of the 20th century, roads were built connecting towns and cities. Federal and state funds to build roads were a major part of the Nevada economy. Tourism was now a booming industry for Reno, with hotels, auto courts, cafés, and service stations providing necessary services for travelers along the Victory and Lincoln Highways.

Nevada's marriage and divorce laws were established in 1861 by the territorial legislature, with a six-month residency period and less strict requirements than in other states. Most states had laws that made it difficult to dissolve a marriage. With the new modes of transportation, Nevada became a marriage and divorce destination. Reno, depending on the divorce industry, lowered the residency requirement to three months in 1927, and then to six weeks in 1931, to ease the economic strain of the Great Depression. The quickie marriage industry brought more people to Nevada, but the residency requirement for divorce had a greater financial impact.

The 1864 state constitution included an anti-gambling law, but it was not enforced. Gambling was legalized in 1869, with numerous technical changes in the law until 1910, when it was again declared illegal. Gaming, meaning the playing of games such as poker and roulette for money, still took place in the back rooms of saloons, going underground until it was declared legal again in 1931. Casinos began to enlarge and to advertise—new for the gaming industry. By the 1940s, gaming was a major economic force in Nevada.

The train, the automobile, and later the plane made it possible for Reno to develop the gambling, divorce, marriage, and tourism industries. While known for these industries, Reno grew into a stable, thriving community and a fine place to live. By the early 1900s, Reno developed from a small railroad town to become the state's financial and industrial center. The University of Nevada was the only four-year college in the state during the time period covered within this book, and all references to it will be to the University of Nevada. From its early days,

Reno supported churches, schools, social, and fraternal organizations, along with numerous community-based activities like parades, theater, rodeos, and county fairs. During the period of this book, Reno's population grew steadily from 1,035 in 1870 to about 25,000 in 1945.

From its humble beginnings as Lake's Crossing, Reno has truly become "the Biggest Little City in the World." We hope you will find learning about the history of Reno, through these remarkable images, as interesting as we found it was for us to research and present it to you.

On July 4, 1911, Washoe County celebrated its 50th anniversary in Reno with a pageant to honor Nevada's history and people. Old pioneers of the state (above) who had crossed the western United States in wagons and on foot in the 1850s were honored. A reception was held at Elk's Hall, where a "Reunion Roll" (now in the Nevada Historical Society archives) was signed and this photograph taken. A band played, "Auld Lang Syne" and "America" were sung by the Double Quartette, talks were given, and Gov. Tasker Oddie awarded the loving cup to the oldest pioneer, David R. Jones. (WA-3408.)

One

FORMING A TOWN

THE 1800s

From the time gold was discovered in California in 1849, emigrants camped along the Truckee River east of the Sierra. By 1859, Charles Fuller had built a bridge and log hotel along the Truckee River in an area known for its water, game, and grass. In 1861, he acquired a toll road franchise from the Nevada Territorial Legislature. This diminutive hotel, which hangs at the Nevada Historical Society in Reno, depicts the hotel and bridge. (WA-1282.)

In 1859, the Comstock Lode, the largest silver strike in the world, was discovered at the site of Virginia City, 20 miles to the south of the Fuller's bridge. The "Rush to Washoe" attracted thousands of fortune seekers from California and elsewhere. From 1859 through 1877, Virginia City and its surrounding mines affected the economy of the area positively, stimulating agriculture and livestock development, requiring timber and freighting. Nevada's population jumped from 6,857 in 1860 to 42,491 in 1870, with almost 25,000 in the Virginia City area. New technologies were developed to support the Comstock such as Deidesheimer's square-set timber system to shore up the deep mines, and the V-flume (at left), used to bring timber (not people) from the Sierra to the valley floor. (ST-1712, WA-NY *Illustrated Times*, 1879.)

Construction of the Central Pacific Railroad east from Sacramento towards Reno began in January 1863. With an elevation gain of 7,017 feet to reach the Donner summit, and the difficulty of carving the route through the granite hills of the Sierra, it took almost five years to reach Nevada. By 1868, the Central Pacific Railroad was making its way east toward Lake's Crossing. (RR-17.)

Early in 1868, the Central Pacific officials looked ahead of the eastward progress of railroad construction to select a desirable site for a station in western Nevada. Quoting from the April 23, 1868, issue of the newspaper from Auburn, California, *Stars and Stripes*, "The name of the new town on the CPRR at the junction of the branch road to Virginia City, in Nevada, is Reno, in honor of General Reno." Jesse L. Reno (shown at right) was a Civil War general killed leading the Union 9th Corps at Fox's Gap on South Mountain in Maryland. (BIO-R-138.)

RENO!

VIRGINIA STATION,

—ON THE—

PACIFIC RAILROAD!

AUCTION SALE OF TOWN LOTS

—IN—

THIS NEWLY LOCATED TOWN

WILL-TAKE PLACE ON

SATURDAY, MAY 9, 1868.

THIS SALE WILL AFFORD A GRAND OPPORtunity for favorable investments in town lots suitable for all kinds of business and trades. The depot being permanently located at this point will give the town of RENO a commanding position of vast importance to secure the trade of Nevada and that portion of California lying east of the Sierras, and will be the natural market for the produce of the rich agricultural valleys north.

Situated on the Truckee River, affording waterpower unsurpassed in the United States, and where the VIRGINIA AND TRUCKEE RAILROAD connects with the PACIFIC, it is unnecessary to enumerate the many advantages this town will possess as the center of immense milling and manufacturing operations.

The sale will take place on the ground, where, prior thereto, a plot of the same can be seen and information in relation to terms obtained, on applying to

D. H. HASKELL, Agent.

Reno, Lake's Bridge, Truckee River, April 30th, 1868.

By 1861, Myron Lake owned Fuller's property and the toll road franchise for the bridge. He built a gristmill on the north side of the Truckee River and a stronger bridge, renaming it Lake's Crossing. By 1868, Lake owned a large section of land directly in the path of the oncoming railroad. Lake profited from his tolls, charging $1 for a loaded wagon, and 50¢ for a horse and buggy. Myron Lake deeded 160 acres of land to the railroad to ensure that a train station would be built at Lake's Crossing. He did not give it away—he bargained for $200 in gold coins and property on the four corners of the bridge. An advertisement announced the May 9, 1868, auction of Reno town lots. The announcement states the Central Pacific meets the Virginia and Truckee in Reno, which did not actually happen until 1872. (WA-1307.)

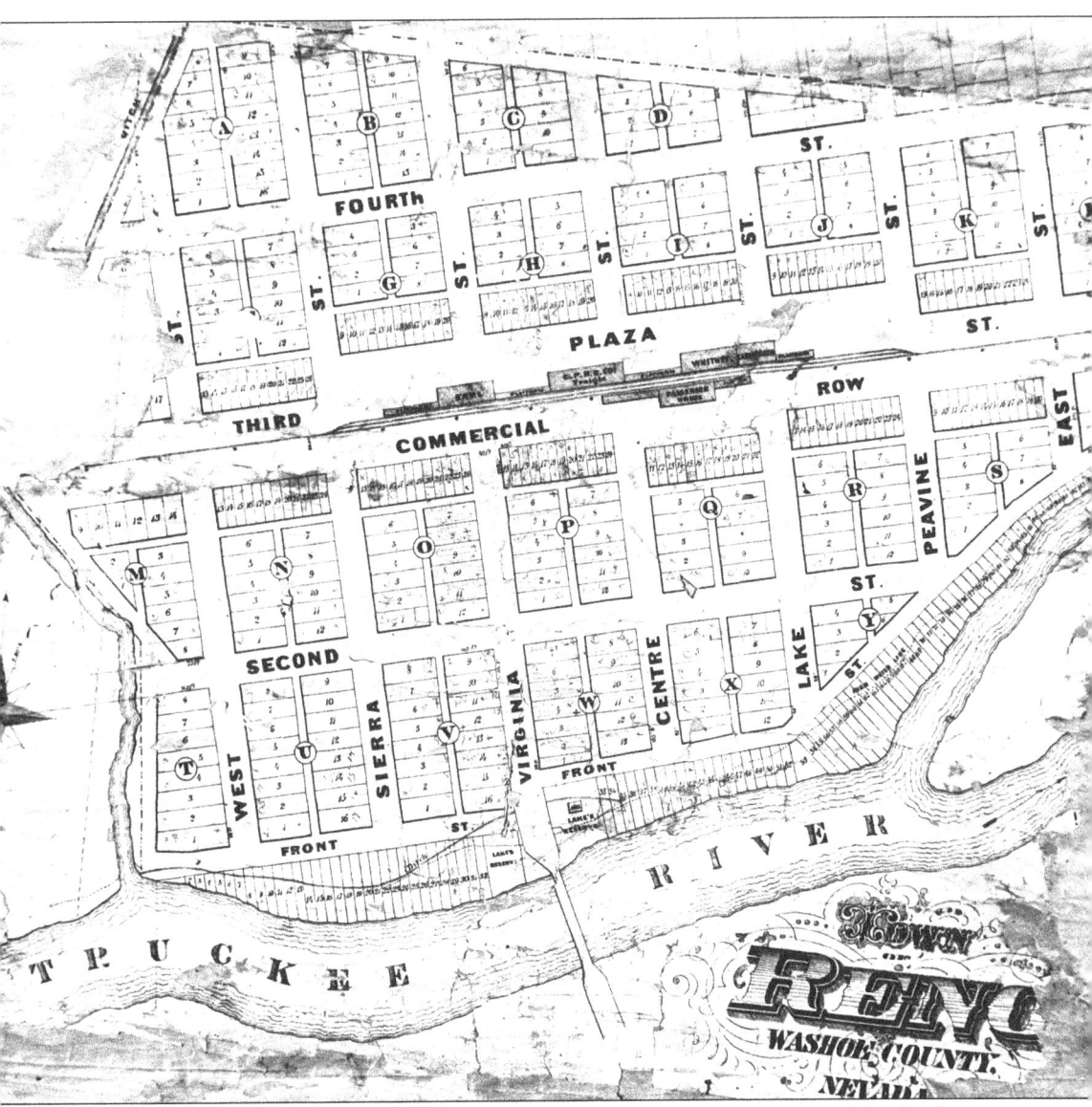

Charles Crocker, superintendent of construction for the Central Pacific Railroad, had Lake's 160 acres surveyed and divided into 400 lots under the first Reno town plan in 1868. The town was fronted along the Truckee River on the south for one-half mile and extended northward from the bank for a little more than a quarter-mile to Fourth and Fifth Streets. West Street was the western border and East Street the eastern border. There was a substantial Midwestern-style central plaza where the trains came through town. More than 1,000 people came to Reno for the May 9 auction, and 70 lots sold for amounts up to $1,000. At the end of the day, only a quarter of the lots had been sold and Central Pacific considered the auction a failure. Even so, the wisdom of selecting Reno as a station site was evident as soon as regular railroad traffic from Sacramento made the new town a major supply center for the Comstock. (WA-1308.)

The pace of building in Reno was frantic, with shacks, shanties, and businesses appearing overnight. Less than a week after the auction, 13 buildings had been erected, and at the end of a month, 100 buildings were completed or under construction. Virginia Street went from the Truckee River north to the Central Pacific freight depot on Commercial Row. The buildings on Virginia Street and Commercial Row consisted mostly of grocery stores and saloons. Myron Lake's Toll Bridge (below) was rebuilt after the 1867 flood. (WA-1279; WA-1271.)

On June 19, 1868, the railroad and telegraph line were completed to Reno. Trains moved about the Reno railroad yard continuously, loading and unloading everything from construction materials to cattle. Reno was now the center of agriculture in the state and the principal Central Pacific station in Nevada. Thriving freight wagon companies carried goods to and from Reno and Virginia City. On August 24, 1872, the Virginia and Truckee Railroad was completed between Reno and Virginia City, ending the prosperity of the freight wagon companies. In 1869, Myron Lake built a larger hotel and trading post on his land south of the Truckee River, naming it Lake House. (RR-101, WA-1281.)

The first newspaper, the *Crescent*, began operation in Reno on July 4, 1868. The move of that paper from Washoe City, where it had been called the *Eastern Slope*, reflected the population shift from Washoe City to Reno. In November 1870, Reno acquired its second paper, the *Nevada State Journal*, now the oldest continuing newspaper in Nevada. The *Reno Evening Gazette* began publication in March 1876 in Myron Lake's gristmill, sometimes referred to as "Old Alhambra," and is still being published today as the *Reno Gazette-Journal*. (WA-*Reno Evening Gazette* headline.)

In 1868, sixteen-year-old Christopher Columbus Powning, selling newspapers on the Central Pacific Railroad, decided to settle in Reno. When the *Nevada State Journal* began in 1870, he became a printer's apprentice. By 1874, the 22-year-old owned the *Journal* and was editor until 1890. Powning was elected state senator, developed Powning's Addition (an early housing development), and was an owner of the Reno Water, Land, and Light Company. He died in 1898 at the age of 46. (BIO-P-230.)

Students first attended school in the basement of Myron Lake's gristmill, called Alhambra Hall, at First and Virginia Streets. In 1869, they moved to Reno's first school, the Riverside School (above) at First and Sierra Streets; it served as both schoolhouse and temporary church for many local denominations. Student enrollment increased so rapidly that another room was soon added, and in 1877, a third room was built. In 1878, Central School (at right) was built at West and Fifth Streets, housing elementary students on the lower floor and Reno High School students on the second floor. (ED-284; ED-313.)

By April 1871, Reno successfully filed lawsuits to move the Washoe County seat from Washoe City to Reno. Myron Lake offered one acre of land, $2,500 in seed money, and water rights, to build a courthouse on South Virginia Street, beside his Lake House. A brick, two-story courthouse was completed in January 1873. Among the duties of the county officials were the care of the indigent ill, the condition of the Virginia Street Bridge, and running the county jail. In 1900, Washoe County officials pose on the steps of the Washoe County Courthouse. From left to right are (seated) D. B. Boyd (county treasurer), C. H. Stoddard (auditor-recorder), Judge John Orr, and Judge W. H. A. Pike; (standing, front right) T. F. Moran (district attorney), George Fogg (deputy county clerk), and Wm. S. Beard (assistant county assessor); (standing, back) Albert G. Ayres (assistant district attorney), Deputy Sheriff Wm. Maxwell, Joe Hogan (assistant auditor-recorder), Mrs. Schwalter and Joe Lozano (court reporters), Judge C. E. Mack, Wm. Fogg (county clerk), and George Davies (deputy county assessor). (WA-1427; WA-1365.)

In 1872, the county commissioners declared Myron Lake's bridge to be a free bridge, ending his toll business. In 1875, the county commissioners decided to replace the weakened wooden bridge on Virginia Street with a more sturdy iron bridge, completed in August 1877. (WA-3979.)

The Depot Hotel was built along the Central Pacific train lines in 1879, after the previous structure burned. The hotel was convenient for train passengers, offering a restaurant, baggage handling, and a ticketing area in the hotel. This hotel burned in 1889 and was replaced by a brick building. (WA-Reno Depot South.)

Fire was a constant threat in early Reno. The town was composed of hastily constructed wooden structures, with the dry climate and frequent high winds exacerbating the situation. Even after 99 downtown buildings burned to the ground in October 1873, two years elapsed before an organized fire department was created. Reno Engine House No. 1 was established on November 10, 1875, and in 1879, it was moved to a site on the plaza owned by the Central Pacific Railroad (above). On March 2, 1879, with almost hurricane-strength winds, a dwelling behind the Masonic Lodge at Sierra Street and Commercial Row caught fire. Using only a steamer and a hand engine, fire crews and volunteers were unable to save the town. As a result, 10 city blocks were destroyed. Within a few months, Reno had rebuilt. The brick Masonic lodge, with hardware store (below), constructed in 1872, was saved and is the oldest surviving commercial building in Reno. A city ordinance required future buildings to be made of brick. (WA-3005, 1883; WA-3335.)

Gus Koppe's stagecoach waited outside the Lake House (later the Riverside Hotel) to take people to Virginia City. In 1863, Geiger and Tilton opened a toll road from Steamboat to Virginia City. Its sharp descent, including hairpin turns and steep slopes, made it impractical for heavy loads, but it was popular for stagecoaches. Drivers had to slow in places, making these spots ideal locations for robberies. (WA-1491.)

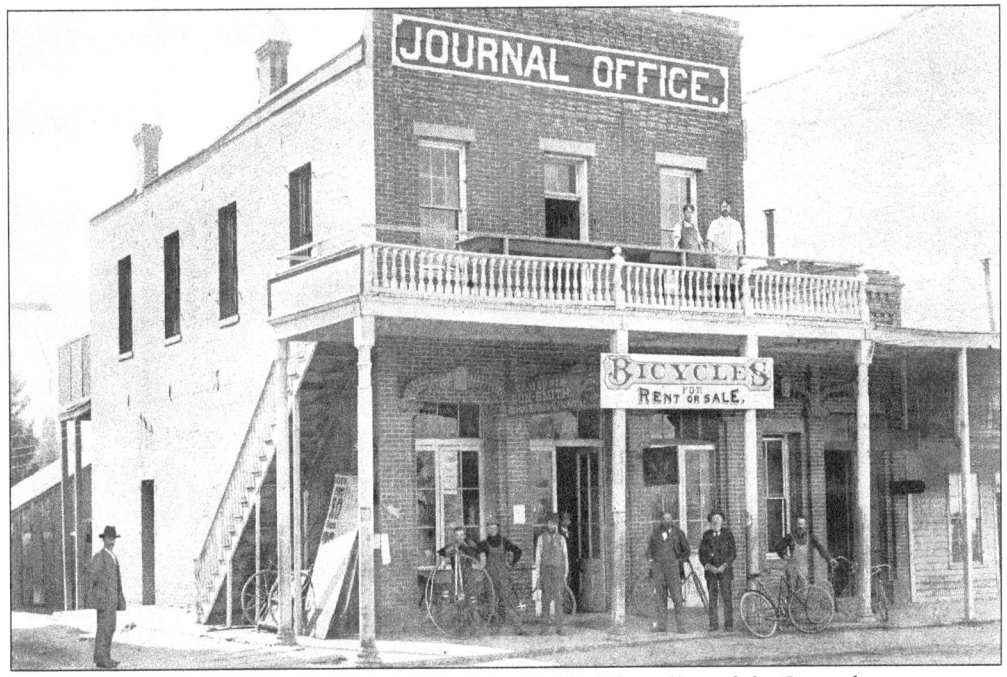

Bicycles were essential for getting around Reno quickly. The office of the *Journal*, a newspaper, was upstairs, and the bicycle shop downstairs had bicycles for sale or rent. The big front-wheel bicycle, also known as the "ordinary bicycle," was popular between 1870 and the 1880s. The "safety bicycle," with two equal-sized wheels, appeared in the late 1880s. (WA-1827.)

In 1880, the Golden Eagle Hotel (above) was moved 13 miles from Crystal Peak to Reno. *Thompson and West History of Nevada*, published in 1881, stated Reno had more than 100 businesses in 1879, including four groceries, six meat markets, four livery stables, three large hotels, seven small hotels, 15 saloons, 12 attorneys, a number of restaurants, flour mills, a brewery, quartz mill, soap factory, tannery, theater, and five churches. By 1890, patrons on foot and in carriages stopped at the new post office (below), on Virginia Street next to the Washoe County Bank at Second and Virginia Streets, to collect mail, converse, and learn the events of the day. (WA-1582; WA-1469.)

Two
BECOMING A CITY
THE EARLY 1900s

By 1878, the Virginia City mines were playing out. Nevada's population dropped from 62,000 in 1880 to 42,000 in 1900. While the state was in an economic depression, Reno became the state's financial and industrial center. The early 1900s brought significant changes to Reno's downtown. Shown in this 1920s photograph are the 1905 Virginia Street Bridge, the 1906 Masonic temple (left), and the 1908 post office (right). Compare this image to the two photographs on page 16, the same views of Virginia Street. (WA-2198.)

MINING NEWS OF THE WEEK

Tonopah Union Strikes Rich Ore Body.

The depressed economy of Nevada changed after 1900, when gold and silver were discovered near Tonopah. In 1902, gold was discovered near what became the town of Goldfield—a boom town in this 1907 photograph below, but almost a ghost town today. The Tonopah and Goldfield mining booms drew 50,000 people to the state. Reno was again the transportation hub for a mining boom, and Reno's population grew from 4,500 in 1900 to 10,867 in 1910. (ESM-42.)

Nevada's first public library, the Carnegie Library, was built in 1904 on South Virginia Street just south of the Truckee River. The library opened with $15,000 donated by Andrew Carnegie on land donated to the city by the Lake family. City hall, built in 1906, is on the left, across the Truckee River. The library remained in service until 1930, when it was moved to the State Building and became the Washoe County Library. (WA-Reno Carnegie.)

The current Virginia Street Bridge was built in 1905 and is the oldest functioning bridge in Reno and one of the first reinforced concrete bridges in Nevada. Because of its design and history, the bridge was placed in the National Register of Historic Places in 1980. The 1906 Riverside Hotel is on the left of the bridge. (WA-1545.)

Reno's second Masonic temple was completed in late 1906 on the north side of the Truckee River at Virginia Street. As in most Masonic buildings, the upper floors contained the Masonic offices and the temple, while the street level was used for commercial purposes. In 1946, the first floor was remodeled to compete with retail businesses in the new Mapes Hotel. The Masonic temple was damaged by fire in 1965 and the front was rebuilt. (WA-Reno, Masonic Temple, 1927.)

Built in 1908, at the corner of Virginia and First Streets, the Federal Office Building and Post Office was a grand redbrick neoclassical structure. Many divorce-seekers received mail in care of general delivery at the post office. The building served as a post office until 1934. It was demolished in late 1945 to make way for a high-rise hotel casino that would revolutionize the gaming industry. (WA-1468.)

The Washoe County Courthouse at 117 South Virginia Street was the first solo commission for architect Frederic DeLongchamps, who won the courthouse design competition in 1909. His Beaux-Arts plan incorporated the 1873 courthouse in the design and was completed in 1910. DeLongchamps designed both additions, the first in the 1940s of matching wings, and the second in 1963 to add the five-story modernist-style structure on the rear, completely enclosing the 1873 courthouse. (WA-1437.)

The 1904 Carnegie Library on Virginia Street was replaced by a new post office (above) in 1934. Architect Frederic DeLongchamps designed the post office, considered to be one of the finest art moderne buildings in Nevada. Constructed during the Great Depression with the help of the Civil Works Administration, the exterior is terra-cotta, incised to resemble quarried stone. The first-floor lobby has spectacular highly ornamented, dark marble walls accented with cast aluminum. (WA-Virginia Street Bridge.)

The first arrivals in what is now northern Nevada came by foot, by horse, and later by wagon—the main means of transportation until the arrival of the train. In 1906, Frank Brothers Wine and Liquor wagon (above) was loaded for distribution to customers. A livery stable was an important business in every town when the horse was the main means of transportation. T. K. Hymer's Truckee Livery and Feed Stable at Second and Sierra Streets was built in 1869 and burned in 1903. (WA-1728; WA-1944.)

The first trolley service in Nevada began between Reno and Sparks. The Nevada Transit Company's first run was on November 24, 1904 (above). The route ran from Fourth and Lake Streets in Reno to the Southern Pacific Roundhouse in Sparks. The route was extended to Sierra Street south and then to Virginia Street. Later an extension was built to Keystone Avenue. The Nevada Interurban ran from Second and Virginia Streets to Moana Lane from 1907 to 1920. The Nevada Transit Company trolleys ceased operation in 1927, unable to compete with the automobile. (WA-1910.)

Chism's Ice Cream Dairy, established by Ed Chism in 1905, is shown selling treats from a horse-drawn wagon in 1910. The dairy supplied cafés, hotels, and stores. Chism Dairy and Bottling Company celebrated its 100th anniversary in 2005. (WA-1696.)

This lodging house, originally known as the Lake House, was built by Myron Lake in 1869. Lake died in 1884, and the Lake family sold the hotel in 1896. This photograph of a Fourth of July celebration clearly shows "Riverside" on the end of the wooden building. In 1896, Harry Gosse took over as manager of the Riverside and operated the hotel for 26 years. He obtained legal ownership in 1906. Between 1901 and 1906, Gosse built a new brick hotel in increments, keeping the older hotel open. The majority of the new chateau-esque version of the Riverside was completed by 1906, just as easy access to transportation brought the first divorce trade to Reno. (WA-1492; WA-1526.)

Tragedy struck when the beautiful Riverside Hotel burned to the ground on March 15, 1922. The fire started in the basement and quickly consumed the structure, leaving only a smoldering brick skeleton. Thankfully, no one was killed. Harry Gosse attempted to rebuild but his insurance was inadequate. In 1924, he sold the property to George Wingfield for $70,000. Wingfield hired architect Frederic DeLongchamps to design a new Riverside. In 1927, Wingfield opened the six-story, Period Revival hotel and casino. In 1950, DeLongchamps designed a three-story wing containing a swimming pool, banquet room, and theater/restaurant. The Riverside closed in the 1980s and was vacant until Sierra Arts purchased the building in 1997. It now houses 35 artists' lofts on the upper floors and retail space on the ground floor. (WA-1516; WA-1550.)

The 1902 American Metropolitan Steam Fire Engine was Reno's third steam pumper. Replacing the 1876 LaFrance steamer as Engine No. 1, the 1902 served Reno for more than 20 years. The last big fire it pumped on was the Riverside Hotel fire in 1922. It is now owned by the Firefighters Historical Steamer Society in California and participates annually in the Tournament of Roses Parade. (WA-3096.)

From the 1890s until 1917, horses pulled the apparatus of the Reno Fire Department (RFD). In 1905, RFD had a horse-drawn hook and ladder truck. In 1908, a brick fire station was built at Center and Ryland Streets, designed for horses with stalls and haylofts. In 1917, RFD bought its first motorized fire apparatus, two Seagrave chemical engines, and the Southside Station (above) was phased out. (WA-3097.)

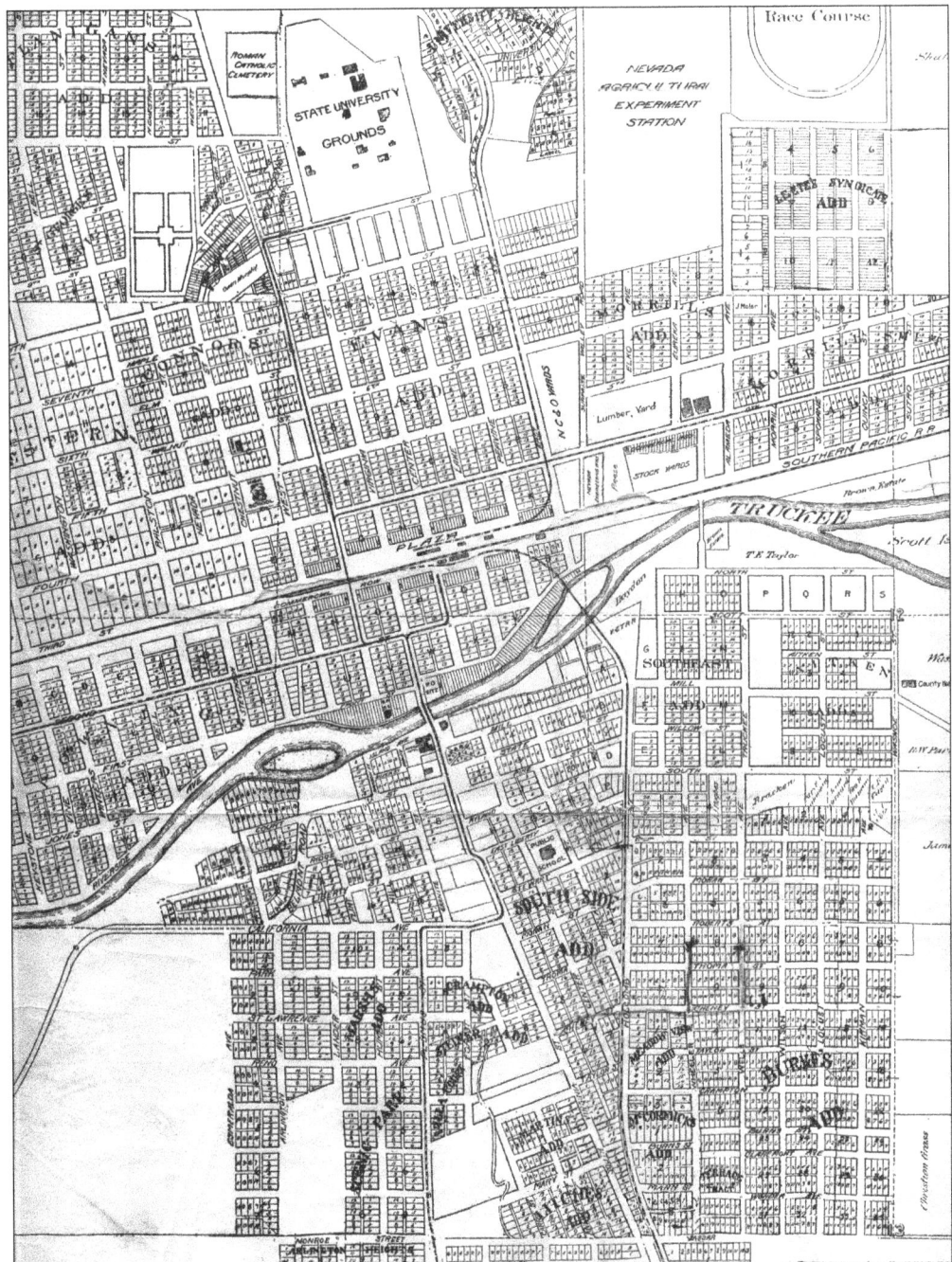

The growth of Reno is obvious in this 1907 Reno street map. The 1868 plat map (on page 15) is contained within the four streets north of the Truckee River. Expansion includes the University of Nevada on the north. Among the first housing developments, the Powning Addition is located on the left just north of the river. Additions (or tracts) were laid out to the immediate north and south of the city, and their names can be seen written across town blocks on the map. The Virginia and Truckee Railroad track leaves the central plaza, crosses the Truckee River, and proceeds south on Holcomb. (Reno Map 1907 b.)

The central part of 1908 Reno is shown with this aerial photograph by George Lawrence—famous for his San Francisco earthquake photograph—done with a system of kites flying at 1,000 feet holding a 46-pound camera. Lawrence positioned the camera with its 22-inch by 55-inch roll of film about 400 feet above the ground on the kite cable. From 600 feet to 1,000 feet, box kites were spaced 50 feet apart to maintain the height of the camera. To the right of the picture, the 1905 Virginia Street Bridge is flanked by the 1906 Masonic temple on the left of the bridge and the 1906 Riverside Hotel on the right. At the top left of the picture, the first buildings of the University of Nevada are visible. Belle Isle, a natural island, sits in the middle of the Truckee River. The wooded island was purchased for an amusement park in 1907, and in 1920, George Wingfield acquired the island and donated it to the City of Reno. In summer, the public enjoyed water activities and amusements around the island. In winter, the frozen Truckee River was a playground for ice-skating and ice hockey. (WA-Reno, 1908 aerial.)

The Lake Mansion was built for the Jerome Marsh family in 1876–1877 on land Myron Lake sold to Marsh. Lake repurchased the property in November 1879 but never lived in the house. Jane Lake, Myron Lake's ex-wife, lived in the mansion from 1885 to 1902. In 1971, the house was to be demolished until the community and Washoe Landmark Preservation raised the funds to move the home to a site at the convention center. In 2004, the home again faced destruction, and once again the community came forward with funds. The mansion was moved to a site at Court Street and Arlington Avenue, not far from its original location at California and South Virginia Streets. The Lake Mansion was placed in the National Register of Historic Places on June 29, 1972. (WA-2438, c. 1900, BIO-L-5.)

SECOND AND VIRGINIA STREETS, SHOWING RENO NATIONAL BANK, RENO, NEVADA

A cowboy and a gambler, George Wingfield gained a fortune in the Goldfield mining boom as George Nixon's partner in the Consolidated Mine Company. Wingfield purchased Nixon's bank in 1920, and owned or had controlling interest in 12 banks by 1930, more than half the state's banking assets. He was the richest man in Nevada in the 1920s. Wingfield played an important role in Nevada politics from 1908 until 1932. Controlling both the Republican and Democratic parties from his Reno National Bank building office, it is said that he made sure there was a Republican senator and a Democratic senator from Nevada in Congress for years. When his banks failed, he was forced into bankruptcy in 1935. (WA-1849; BIO-W-367.)

In the early 1900s, people traveled to Reno by train. By the 1920s, automobiles brought even more people, and the need for hotels and living spaces increased dramatically. Reno had more hotels operating in the 1930s and 1940s than one might expect for a town its size, due largely to the growth of gambling, automobile tourism, and the divorce trade. Gov. John Sparks had his Alamo Stock Farm office in the Overland Hotel. The hotel was a busy place; the first floor of the hotel was a restaurant and an assay office. The Overland Hotel lobby was a gathering spot—with spittoons on the floor. The bar was adjacent to the lobby. (WA-1604; WA-1603.)

The Golden Hotel was built in 1906 by Frank Golden Sr. as competition for the Riverside Hotel. Financed by the Wingfield family, the Golden Hotel was taken over by the Wingfields when Frank Golden died in 1914. The hotel catered to a more upscale clientele and was the residency choice of many a divorce seeker. The Golden Hotel bus went to the train depot several times daily to transport clients. Both the Golden Hotel and the Overland Hotel were on this section of Center Street, with the freight off-loading docks at the end of the street. In 1932, the docks were removed, and Center Street continued north to the university. The Wingfield family operated the hotel until 1946. The Golden Hotel burned to the ground in a fire in 1962. (WA-2226a, c. 1930; WA-1584, 1921.)

The first arch, at Virginia Street and Commercial Row, was erected in 1926 as part of the Transcontinental Highways Exposition, celebrating the completion of the coast-to-coast motor routes, the Lincoln and Victory Highways. Following the exposition, the Reno City Council decided to keep the arch as a permanent downtown gateway. In 1929, the winning jingle in a contest to give Reno a slogan for the arch (above) was "The Biggest Little City in the World." In 1935, a green neon arch with only the word "Reno" appeared. The public complained about losing the slogan, and later that year the arch (below) sported a new sign on the original framework with white neon art deco lettering. For the next 30 years, this arch remained the only constant in the growing, bustling "Biggest Little City," while everything around it changed. (WA-8158; WA-2125.)

On New Year's Eve 1963, a modern geometrically shaped Reno arch replaced the 1935 arch. The old arch was moved first to Idlewild Park and then to Paradise Park on Oddie Boulevard. In 1977, the 1963 arch caught fire from the combustion of pigeon droppings, resulting in many humorous stories and jokes. (WA-2134A.)

In 1987, a new Reno arch was dedicated on Virginia Street. In 1990, the 1963 arch was given to Willits, California. In 1994, a movie production company paid to have the 1935 Reno arch restored for the movie *Cobb*. Afterwards, the historic landmark was installed on Lake Street between the Siena Hotel Spa Casino and the National Automobile Museum. (Courtesy Dave Kennedy.)

Between 1890 and 1930, the Basque boardinghouse or *ostatuak* was an important institution for the Basque sheepherders from the Pyrenees region on the border of France and Spain. By the 1900s, Nevada had a substantial Basque population. The hotel keeper or *hoteleros* would find work for recent immigrants on ranches. The *ostatuak* provided familiar food and drink, people who spoke their native language, and a hotel keeper who smoothed the way in America. The herder kept his cherished belongings and his Sunday suit at the *ostatuak*. The earliest recorded Reno Basque hotel is the Commercial Hotel (1904). The Santa Fe on Lake Street and Louis' Basque on Fourth Street were Basque boardinghouses and are still open for business. Perhaps only a dozen former Basque boardinghouses are still open in the West, providing Basque food and music to Basques and non-Basques. (WA-1641, 1954.)

The heart of Reno's "Little Italy" commercial district centered around Lake Street between Second Street and Commercial Row. There were hotels, groceries, a fish market, and a newspaper, all owned by people of Italian descent. The Western commercial-style Mizpah Hotel (shown above) was constructed by the Pincolini family in three stages in 1922, 1925, and 1930. The Reno Public Market was on the street level of the hotel. Sadly, the historic Mizpah burned in 2006. (WA-1642, late 1950s.)

The El Cortez Hotel at Second Street and Chestnut Street (now Arlington Avenue), designed by architect George A. Ferris and son Lehman, was built in 1931. The seven-story structure was the city's tallest building at the time. It was considered a first-class destination hotel for divorcées arriving in Reno. The going rate per night for a room was $6, compared to $2.50 at many other establishments. In 1941, the El Cortez opened the Trocadero Room, an elegant nightclub, cocktail lounge, and gaming room on the first floor. (WA-1647.)

The 12-story Mapes Hotel opened on December 17, 1947, at the southeast corner of First and Virginia Streets, along the Truckee River. It was the first in Nevada to combine a hotel, casino, and entertainment, and it became the prototype for modern hotels and casinos. The Mapes was built especially to offer gaming, rooms and suites, restaurants and bars, and entertainment all under one roof. Its art deco architecture was a style late for the time, because plans for the building were drawn before World War II. Big name entertainers like Sammy Davis Jr. and Frank Sinatra performed in the famous Mapes Sky Room. At the time it was constructed, it was the tallest building in Nevada. The Mapes Hotel closed December 17, 1982 and remained vacant for 18 years. After a long and bitter battle to preserve the building, it was imploded at 8:03 a.m. on Sunday, January 30, 2000. (WA-4356.)

Three

RAILROADS

LINKING THE NATION

The idea for a transcontinental railroad to "shrink the continent and change the whole world" was first proposed in 1832. In 1862, Congress passed the Pacific Railway Act authorizing the Union Pacific Railway Company to build west from Omaha, Nebraska, and the Central Pacific Railroad Company to build east from Sacramento, California. The Oneonta was a Central Pacific Railroad construction locomotive working in the Sierra, shown above in Cisco, California. (RR-36.)

The route of the Central Pacific was selected to tie California to the Union and to connect to gold mining in California and the silver in Nevada's Comstock Lode. Construction of the Central Pacific Railroad and the telegraph line began in Sacramento on January 8, 1863. By the end of 1865, eighty-seven miles of track were laid towards Reno. By November 1866, the track reached Cisco, and Charles Crocker moved operations over the summit to also work from the east side of the Sierra. Three locomotives, 40 train cars, and 40 miles of track were hauled over the summit in sledges. During the heavy winters of 1866–1867 (at left) and 1867–1868, snowplows were used to clear the tracks as snowsheds and tunnels were built. Central Pacific construction trains (below) worked on the railroad track close to Reno in 1868. (RR-5; RR-10.)

Thousands of Chinese were brought from China by the Central Pacific Railroad to work on the construction of the railroad. Their work was essential to the success of the endeavor. The 154 miles of track from Sacramento to Reno was completed on June 19, 1868. The May 10, 1869, joining of the Central Pacific Railroad and the Union Pacific Railroad at Promontory, Utah, (above) with the Central Pacific locomotive *Jupiter* on the left and the Union Pacific No. 119 on the right, brought the wagon train period to a close. In the 1890s, people waited at Reno's Central Pacific depot (below) for passengers to detrain. (RR-125; RR-102.)

Freight shipments from California, destined for Reno, crossed the Sierra over Donner Pass, a route with steep grades, numerous tunnels, and snowsheds. Multiple steam locomotives were needed to make the 2 percent, and occasionally 2.5 percent, grade over Donner Pass. The exhaust and combustion gases caused breathing problems for locomotive crews going through the tunnels and sheds. Southern Pacific had Baldwin Locomotive build a powerful locomotive with the cab at the front, called the Cab-Forward, between 1928 and 1944. The Southern Pacific Cab-Forward 4154 locomotive is an example. The Wells Fargo and Company Express on Commercial Row (below) had V&T tracks in front of the building and Southern Pacific tracks behind for shipping freight and valuables. (RR-165; WA-5499.)

Following World War I, railroads encouraged the public to "see America first." Before airplanes and automobiles, long distance travel was synonymous with trains—and Americans wanted to travel. The train depot was constructed in 1925. In 2005, the depot was restored and a lower level added in the original style of the building. The Southern Pacific Railroad's *City of San Francisco* streamline train left the Reno Depot on its first trial run in 1936. (RR-SPRR Depot; RR-169.)

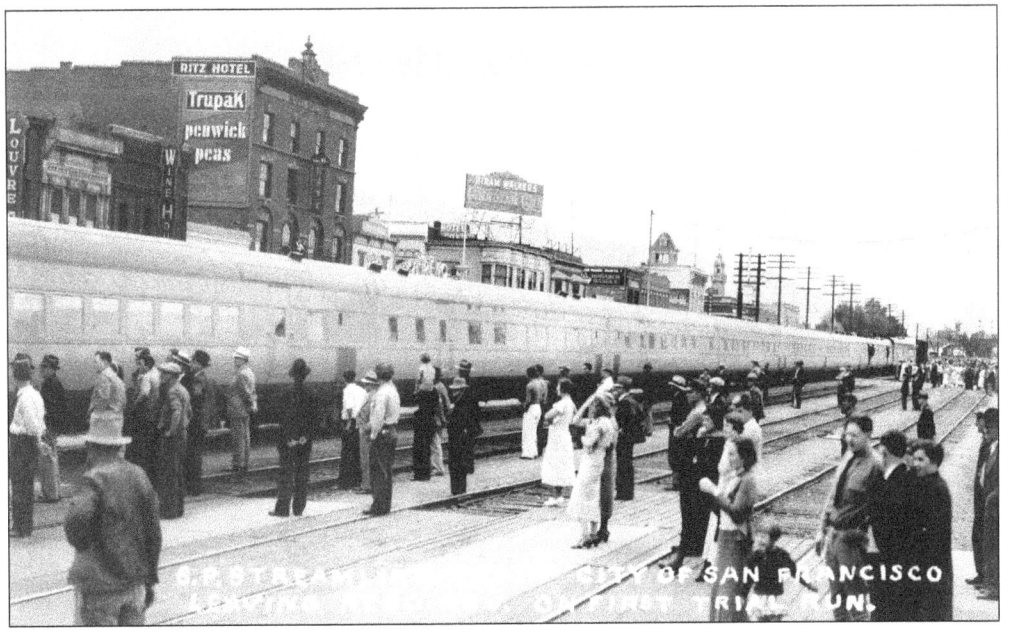

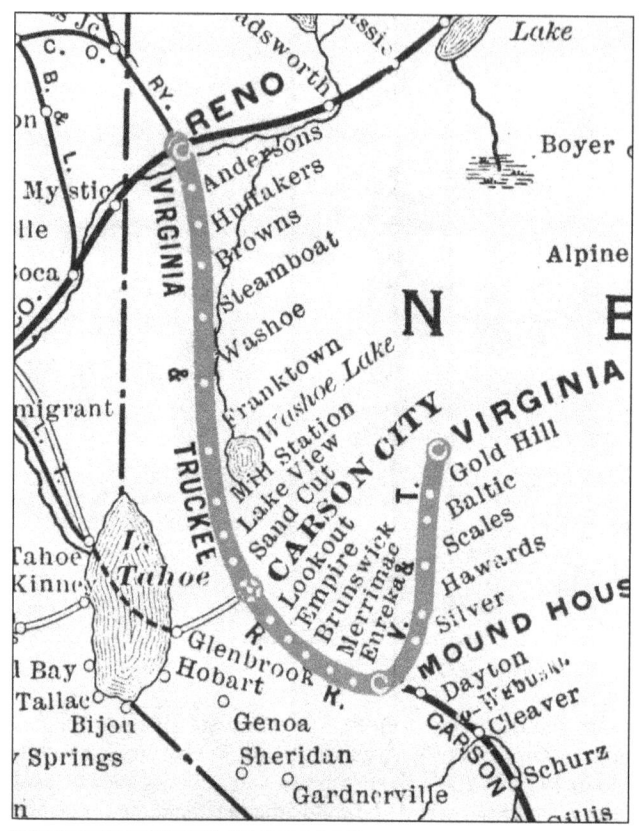

The Virginia and Truckee Railroad (V&T), the most famous short-line railroad in American history, ran from Virginia City to Carson City and on to Reno. The railroad was incorporated in 1867 to serve the mines of the Comstock and to cut the high cost of freighting goods by wagon in and out of Virginia City. The 21-mile standard-gauge line between Carson City and Virginia City was completed on January 29, 1870. There were seven tunnels and an elevation drop of 1,575 feet. The V&T was called the "crookedest railroad in the world" because of the number of twists and turns to get the trains up and down Mount Davidson at the proper angles. An 85-foot-high, 500-foot-long trestle was built across Crown Point Ravine. (WA-V&T Railroad Map; WA-Crown Point Trestle.)

In August 1872, a 31-mile extension of the V&T from Carson City through Franktown, Washoe City, and Steamboat Springs connected the Comstock with transcontinental rail service at Reno. Engine No. 22 crossed a bolted timber bridge (above) over the Truckee in line with Holcomb Avenue bringing the train into Reno. The first Holcomb bridge had 11 trestles in the river's channel and supported a main span of 150 feet. The V&T's Reno engine house and turntable were built on the south side of the Truckee River just before the bridge. The Riverside Mill Company is visible across the river; the mill turned out 100 barrels of flour a day. A V&T train, with Engine No. 11, the *Reno* (below), prepared to depart the depot. (RR-1535; RR-351.)

In 1906, the V&T tracks were extended from Carson City south to Minden. With the poor roads and lack of automobiles, the passenger service was well received. Gov. John Sparks rode from Reno to Carson City regularly from 1903 to 1908. Well-known visitors on the V&T included Presidents Ulysses S. Grant, Rutherford B. Hayes, Teddy Roosevelt, and Herbert Hoover. V&T service from Carson City to Virginia City ended in 1939. The V&T ceased operation in 1950, unable to compete with trucks and automobiles. On May 31, 1950, people gathered for the V&T Railroad's last run ceremony (below). In 2010, thanks to the work of railroad aficionados, tourist trains run the restored V&T line from east of Carson City to and from Virginia City. (WA-V&T RR Ticket; Mulcahy 53.)

The Central Pacific was absorbed into the Southern Pacific in 1899. Some 373 miles of the original Central Pacific line were rebuilt, shortening the line in places. The decision to take Wadsworth, Nevada (above), a division terminal, off the main line was announced in 1902. During the summer of 1904, the terminal was moved just east of Reno. Southern Pacific moved the residents and their homes by train from Wadsworth to the new location. In 1905, the City of Sparks was incorporated by the state legislature and named in honor of John Sparks (at right), rancher and governor of Nevada. Sparks had one of the largest roundhouses in the world during the steam era. Huge steam engines hauled both freight and passengers up the steep grades of the Sierra Nevada. (RR-205, 1899; BIO-S-215.)

Fourth Street's proximity to the Central Pacific tracks, later the Southern Pacific, and the V&T tracks made it a perfect location for warehouses and manufacturers to ship supplies to and from Reno. The Nevada-California-Oregon (N-C-O) Railway was started in 1880 to carry passengers and freight from Reno to and from northeastern California and Oregon. The N-C-O depot (above) was designed by Frederic DeLongchamps in 1910. The locomotive house (below), built in 1889, is the oldest remaining engine house in the state. The N-C-O Railway was considered the longest narrow-gauge railroad, at 238 miles, when it reached Lakeview, Oregon, in 1912. In 1917, N-C-O sold 64 miles of the line and the Reno depot to Western Pacific Railroad, who changed the tracks to standard gauge. From 1917 to 1937, the depot served as a Western Pacific passenger and freight depot. (RR-962; RR-1156.)

Four
NEW MODES OF TRANSPORTATION
AUTOMOBILES AND AIRPLANES

Automobiles and airplanes changed transportation in the United States. With the arrival of the automobile, the driving public demanded better roads in Reno and between communities. In his 1913 *History of Nevada*, Samuel Davis describes Reno's accommodation to the automobile as follows: "Reno is up to date with asphalt and macadamized streets and 36 miles of sidewalks." In 1923, Clark and Henery Construction Company was building a road in Reno. (WA-2352.)

Tasker Oddie, in his 1910 campaign for governor, took an auto tour of the entire state over nearly impassable roads. He recognized the importance of roads for Nevada and was instrumental in promoting improvements. In 1916, Congress passed a law providing for federal/state cooperation in building and financing highways. Between 1919 and 1920, the Nevada road program began by eliminating the worst hazards with horse-drawn scrapers and oiling the gravel roads. A Thomas Flyer and its passengers sit in front of the Reno Stock Brokerage Company in 1906 (above). A shiny new Dodge with driver waits in front of Osen Dodge Motor Sales on Plaza Street between Sierra and Virginia Streets below. (WA-4670; Curtis-122.)

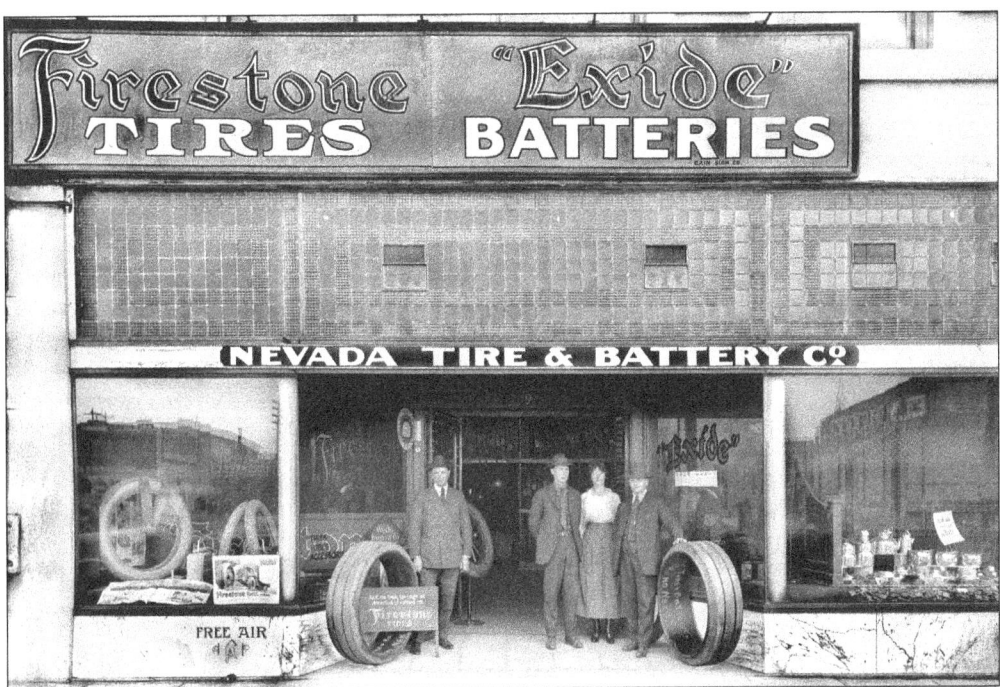

Driving became a national pastime with the arrival of the automobile, and the Sunday drive was a fashionable way to entertain the family. In 1913, Nevada began registering, licensing, and taxing motor vehicles. Of the 1,093 Nevada vehicles registered, 57 were trucks, buses, delivery cars, or taxi cabs. There were 103 makes of vehicles including 212 Fords, 101 Studebakers, 92 Buicks, 61 Willys Overlands, 57 Cadillacs, 52 REOs, and 44 Hupmobiles. Thirty-one women registered vehicles. With the automobile came auto repair shops and related businesses, such as Firestone Tires and Batteries. The first truckload of tires shipped to Nevada arrived at Sierra Auto Supply in 1919. (Curtis-6; Curtis-11.)

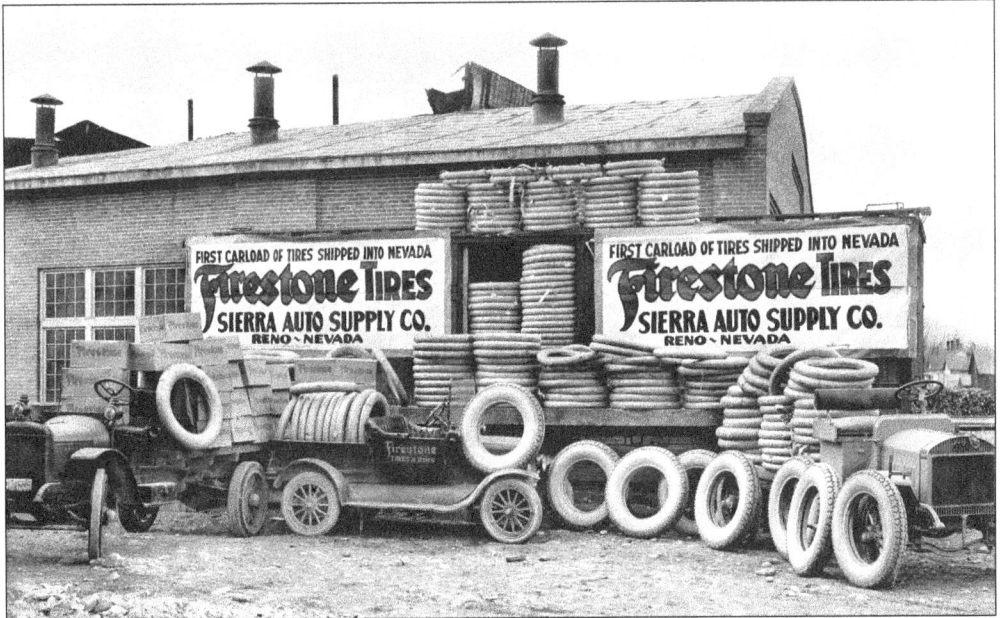

In 1913, Reno was included in the plan for the Lincoln Highway, the first transcontinental road linking New York City and San Francisco. The Lincoln Highway played an important role in the development of cross-country automobile travel. The goal was to improve and connect the roads across the country to form a highway by 1915. The bridge railing, built east of Verdi in April 1914, was the first bridge with the Lincoln Highway name. When the Lincoln and Victory Highways were given numbers instead of names in 1928, the road through Reno on Fourth Street was designated U.S. 40. Travelers on the two-lane road campaigned for a wider highway in the 1940s. Pappy Smith of Harolds Club paid for the billboards. (TRAN-Hwy372; WA-6156.)

In 1927, to celebrate the completion of the Victory and the Lincoln Highways, later U.S. 40 and U.S. 50 respectively, Nevada and California sponsored the Transcontinental Highways Exposition at Idlewild Park in Reno. The arch (above) was built on Virginia Street to celebrate the exposition and dedicated October 23, 1926. The State of California built the California Building (below), in Idlewild Park, as a gift to the people of Nevada. Nevada joined in marking the occasion by constructing the State Building on South Virginia and Mill Streets. The State Building initially had exposition displays but served the community in a multitude of ways, including as a library and the Nevada Historical Society until 1965. (Neal Cobb Collection-Reno Arch-27, Postcard from Dick Stoddard; WA-2827.)

In the early 20th century, Reno reaped the benefits of travelers arriving to gamble, get a divorce, or get married. Mining was no longer the state's largest income producer, and Reno's economy depended on the tourist trade. Before 1920, people relied on the railroads for transportation between cities. As highways were built, people traveled to places by car. The Lincoln and Victory Highways ran along Fourth Street in Reno, offering opportunities for restaurants, hotels, and campgrounds. In 1927, the advertisement urged people to vacation in Reno. (WA-Reno advertisement for city.)

By 1915, America was a country on wheels. Newly constructed roads connected Nevada towns, and thousands of automobiles crossed Nevada annually by 1920. A major east-west highway, the Victory Highway (later called U.S. 40, and even later I-80), crossed the northern part of the state, through Reno, following the emigrant trail. Road building was a major portion of the state's economy. Reno loved a parade, and cars are lined up in front of the Reno National Bank building to enter the parade in this 1918 photograph. A downside of the country's love affair with the automobile was the fact that there were breakdowns. (WA-Reno Virginia Street with parade cars; WA-car outing.)

In 1838, Congress designated all railroads as official postal routes. Mule-drawn covered wagons carried the first regular mail service between Sacramento and Salt Lake City in 1851. Between 1860 and 1861, the Pony Express carried mail across the western United States, with 20 relay stations operating across central Nevada. After the telegraph system replaced the Pony Express in 1861, hand-carried mail traveled by stagecoach. Once the Central Pacific and the Union Pacific were completed across the West in 1869, Reno had railway mail service. Within Reno, mail was moved by horse-drawn Parcel Post wagons. By 1920, the mail was transported by a U.S. Mail car, such as the Essex. (WA-1471; WA-1672.)

The introduction of the airplane in 1903 led to the idea of transporting mail by air. The first flight over the Sierra Nevada (above) was on March 22, 1919. Transcontinental airmail service was established in September 1920, from Omaha, with many stops, including Reno, and then to San Francisco. The first airmail delivery (below), stopping in Reno from Salt Lake City, was on September 11, 1920, flown by pilot J. P. Woodward. The current Washoe County Golf Course on Plumas Street and Urban Road was the site of the U.S. Airmail Service Airport, called Blanchfield Field, established in 1920. (TRAN-ABS-13; WA-1215.)

For the next seven years, government pilots flew 4,200-pound DeHaviland Model 4 biplanes (above) on regular flights over the Sierra Nevada. In 1927, Boeing Air Transport took over the mail contract to and from Blanchfield Field (below). The reliability of the open cockpit, wooden-framed, cloth-covered, wire-bound biplanes was good, but the Sierra pushed them to their limits. Passenger service began in 1927, and at first passengers sat on folding chairs in the open cockpit, sometimes holding the mail on their laps. Boeing upgraded its planes to more powerful, closed-cabin planes that could carry 1600 pounds of mail, express freight, or passengers. These planes ended the pioneer phase of aviation history over the Sierra. (TRAN-ABS-144, TRAN-ABS-125.)

Charles Lindbergh, a 25-year-old airmail pilot, became world famous after his solo nonstop flight from New York to Paris, France, on May 20–21, 1927. On September 19, 1927, Lindbergh landed at Blanchfield Field in his airplane, the *Spirit of St. Louis*, noting that Reno's Blanchfield Field was too small to accommodate even the two-passenger Boeing Model 40a aircraft. As a national hero, he was given a welcoming parade and awarded a testimonial scroll by the City of Reno. (WA-1214.)

In July 1928, Boeing Air Transport purchased a new landing field east of Reno for a stop on the San Francisco-to-Chicago mail run and named it Hubbard Field for pioneer Boeing aviator Eddie Hubbard. United purchased Hubbard Field in 1937, and the City of Reno acquired it in 1953. Today the airfield is known as Reno-Tahoe International Airport. In 1941, passengers deplane from a Douglas Aircraft DC-3 at Hubbard Field (below). (WA-United Airlines.)

Reno Army Air Base was originally assigned to the Second Air Force to train soldiers (above) in the Army Signal Corps. The Ferrying Division of the Air Transport Command (below) assumed command of the base in 1943 until its deactivation in 1945. In April 1948, the 192nd Fighter Squadron of the Nevada National Guard took over the vacant base for training activities. In December 1949, Lt. Croston Stead, a Reno native, lost his life when his P-51 Mustang crashed at the base during a training mission. In January 1951, the base was named Stead Air Force Base (AFB) in his honor. Since 1966, the National Championship Air Races, also known as the Reno Air Races, have been held at Stead AFB. (TRAN-ABS-39; WA-1248.)

Five
SURVIVING THE DEPRESSION
A MARRIAGE AND DIVORCE DESTINATION

Reno was known as the "Divorce Capital of the World" between 1910 and 1970. Newspaper articles, magazines, novels, and several plays were written based on the Reno divorce trade. In Clare Booth Luce's 1936 Broadway play *The Women*, four women are in Reno to shed their mates. Coming to Reno to get a divorce was known as "taking the cure" or getting "Reno-vated," the latter a term coined by newspaper columnist Walter Winchell. (WA-*Reno Divorce* cover-magazine.)

The 1940 magazine, *The Reno Divorce Racket*, carried the article "Taking the Cure." Nevada's marriage and divorce laws were established in 1861 by the first territorial legislature. The residency period for a bona fide citizen was six months, less strict than in other states. In Nevada, the courts did not demand extensive evidence of wrongdoing. From the early 1900s, Reno's economy relied on the divorce industry. By 1910, hundreds were traveling to Reno by train every year to establish residency for divorce. Beul's cartoon ran in the *Reno Evening Gazette* in 1909. (WA-*Reno Divorce Racket*, "Taking the Cure"; WA-Divorce cartoon by Beul.)

America's sweetheart Mary Pickford (at right) came to Nevada in 1920 to divorce her first husband and marry actor Douglas Fairbanks. The divorces of the rich and famous, including British Lord Russell in 1899 and U.S. Steel president William Corey in 1906, drew attention to Reno as a divorce center. The Reno divorce industry grew when California added a one-year residency requirement before a final decree. In 1913, through the efforts of members of the Progressive Party in Nevada, Gov. Tasker Oddie recommended that the six-month residency law be changed to one year, and the legislature complied. In 1915, businesses hurt by the law lobbied successfully for a change back to six-months. (WA-Pickford newspaper photograph.)

Nevada State Journal
April 5, 1981

With the possibility of quick divorces in Paris and Mexico City, Nevada reduced the divorce residency requirement to three months in 1927. During the Great Depression, Nevada lawmakers hoped to improve Nevada's economy by decreasing the residency requirement to six weeks in 1931. Boxer Jack Dempsey (at left, center) came to Reno for a divorce in 1931. (WA-Dempsey-divorce.)

The several-thousand people who came to the state annually to obtain divorces left substantial sums of money, materially easing the effects of the Depression. During the 1930s, more than 30,000 divorces were granted at the Washoe County Courthouse. That meant 30,000 people who rented living quarters, ate, and played in Reno over a six-week period. Today Reno would call it equivalent to 126,000 room-nights annually. Although the gambling bill was of much greater long-term importance to the state, the six-week divorce law was of more immediate economic benefit. The Thomas Café (above) on Center Street was known as the divorcées' favorite place to eat in Reno. The cartoon below comments on the state of marriage and offers six weeks in Nevada as the cure. (WA-Reno, Thomas Café; WA-5538.)

According to Reno folklore, numerous newly divorced people, upon leaving the nearby courthouse, threw their wedding rings from the Virginia Street Bridge into the Truckee River. Many postcards with a divorce theme were sent home to friends and family. Both of these postcards are from the Lew Hymers Collection. Lew Hymers caricatures, compiled in his book called *Seen About Town*, were a popular feature in the *Nevada State Journal* in the 1930s and 1940s. A dude cowboy carries luggage for a newly arrived divorcée in the postcard known as "6 Weeks." (Hymers Collection, Divorce Postcard, "Tossing Ring"; Hymers Collection, "6 Weeks in Reno.")

With a six-week residency requirement, Reno accommodated its visitors by building hotels and alley homes, converting ranches to dude ranches, and homes to boardinghouses. The Riverside and the El Cortez Hotels were built for the divorce trade. Residents partitioned their homes to rent out rooms. Some residents rented out their homes to divorcées and moved elsewhere. Other divorcées stayed in campgrounds. Monte Cristo Dude Ranch (above) in 1930 and Valley Ranch (below) in 1940 were typical of the dude ranches where a divorcée might stay. The hosts guaranteed the guests would enjoy themselves. (WA-6562; WA-Valley Ranch.)

Nevada was criticized for its easy divorce and gambling laws, and it gained the name "Sin City." Some people regarded it as sinful that judges in Nevada courts dissolved marriages so easily, and Reno developed a bad reputation in parts of the country. A 1934 article on Nevada's divorce law in *Fortune Magazine* offered this description of the town: "Reno lies in Nevada's western corner, 10 miles from California. Population 18,500. Elevation 4,500 feet. Reputation: bad." In the 1930s, the Lazy ME (above) sent its dude cowboys to pick up guests at the depot. Around town, the Lazy ME's nickname was the "Lay Me Easy." About 1950, the Pyramid Lake Ranch (below) welcomed and entertained divorcées. (WA-6637; WA-9165.)

Although the divorce business received a great deal more notoriety, Nevada was also building a reputation as a marriage center. Marriages outnumbered divorces in both the 1920s and 1930s. Since those who came to be married stayed only a short while, the time spent by those seeking a divorce had a greater impact on the state's economy. In 1927, Nevada benefited when California added a three-day waiting period for marriage licenses, and later required a premarital medical exam. Nevada became a favorite place for weddings—with no waiting period, no physical exam, and no blood test. Thousands came each month. In 1910, they came by train. In the 1920s, they came by car. In the 1940s, they also came by air. The Hitching Post Wedding Chapel (above) and the Sunset Wedding Chapel (below) were among the chapels that opened near the courthouse, the bus station, and casinos. (WA-Reno Hitching Post; WA-9439.)

Six
RENO OR BUST
THE GAMING INDUSTRY

Gaming is as old as Nevada. Mississippi River gamblers followed the soldiers to the Mexican-American War, then to the California Gold Rush and on to Washoe and the Comstock. The Willows (formerly Rick's Resort, where fighter Jack Johnson trained in 1910), a plush casino and dinner house on what is now Mayberry Road, operated an elegant speakeasy and gaming operation long before gambling was legalized in 1931. (WA-The Willows roulette.)

Gaming grew up with the state of Nevada. California-bound emigrants set up games of chance, and gamblers prospered in the early camps because miners liked to gamble. Technically, gambling was illegal, but the Utah Territory did not prosecute. After Nevada became a state in 1864, the legislature passed an anti-gambling law. Initially it was not enforced, but by 1866, licenses were required. The Palace Club and Hotel opened on Commercial Row and Center Street in 1888. The Palace, the largest gaming club in the state at the time, burned (above) on March 1, 1909, but was rebuilt in time to serve as headquarters for the Johnson-Jeffries fight on July 4, 1910. The Palace continued to offer gambling (below) and operated until 1979. (DS-WA-1 Commercial Row, Palace Club fire, Dave Stafford Collection; WA-3565.)

In 1869, Nevada law permitted gamblers to operate openly. Between 1869 and 1909, gaming law changed the age requirements and outlawed certain games, locations, and hours. Women's groups and religious organizations succeeded in having gambling declared illegal in 1910. Customers were busy at the Louvre on the last night of legal gambling in 1910. (WA-3553.)

Despite the new law, gambling continued to operate in the back rooms of saloons. Before the 1930s, there were no casinos, and no respectable woman would enter a saloon. The Palace and the Bank Club offered high stakes games, played late at night, with bootleg liquor and a bouncer at the door. Reno mayor E. E. Roberts was reelected in 1931 on a campaign to drop controls on gambling, divorce, and alcohol. In March 1931, the Nevada legislature again legalized gambling. County governments were authorized to collect a tax from the gaming operators. The national prohibition on alcohol was repealed in December 1933. In Reno, work began to enlarge the city's biggest casino, the Bank Club, and to remodel others. (WA-3573.)

After the repeal of the gambling law, Reno mayor E. E. Roberts stated, "now we can do lawfully what Nevada has always done under cover." For almost a decade after gaming was legalized in 1931, it retained a frontier, back room atmosphere. Raymond "Pappy" Smith (at left) and his son Harold Smith opened a small casino on Virginia Street in 1935 and changed forever how casinos in Nevada would operate. For a short time, Smith became well-known by running a roulette wheel with live mice. In another gimmick (below), Smith and Dolores Rose stood by the roulette wheel with their live elephant. (BIO-S-165; WA-6070.)

The little casino grew slowly during its first five years, until World War II gave it the boost it needed. The Smiths began an advertising campaign with Harolds Club signs located all over the United States and the world (at right). Previously, advertising was not considered good business for gaming. Gaming operators feared it would give moralists ammunition against gambling. Harolds Club created newspaper ads with "Pioneer Nevada" stories. Western history buffs loved it, and Harolds Club was expanded again and again. By the end of World War II, 5,000 people a day entered the club, and by the end of the 1940s, Harolds Club welcomed 20,000 people a day. The success of Harolds Club encouraged others to advertise—after all, gaming was legal in Nevada and should be advertised like any other business. (WA-3545; WA-3542.)

The legend at the top of the Harolds Club mural reads: "Dedicated in all humility to those who blazed the trail." The 40-foot-by-70-foot mural was erected on the side of Harolds Club in October 1949. The Smith family commissioned artist Theodore McFall to paint the scene. Sgt. Claude Johnson sculpted the steel and fired the colors for the 180 pieces of porcelain enamel-painted steel, mirrors, and moving parts that make up the mural. The design honors the early pioneers who crossed the Great Plains in covered wagons. The astonishing detail includes a wagon train, pioneers at a campsite, a campfire burning, and a cascading waterfall. The mural was removed in 1999 and is now on display adjacent to the Reno Livestock Center at the Reno Rodeo grounds. (WA-Reno, Harolds Club with mural.)

William Harrah was the second person to change the face of gaming in Reno. He opened Harrah's Tango Club on Douglas Alley (below) in 1939. The club was popular, and in 1942 Harrah opened a casino, the Blackout Bar, on North Virginia. His business benefitted from being near Harolds Club and the similarity of their names. (BIO-H-291.)

Gaming moved from the back room to Main Street in the 1940s. Neon lights advertised gaming establishments. Slots remained in the casinos, but were also in drugstores, grocery stores, and cafes. In Elko, a casino operator brought in big name live entertainment and drew huge crowds. Reno and Las Vegas soon followed suit, and a new entertainment industry was born. (WA-2228.)

The Palace Club was full of customers in 1942 (above). After World War II ended in 1945, wartime restrictions on travel ended. People flocked to Nevada, and the gaming industry grew. Reno's casinos flourished as new businesses opened and older establishments expanded. In this 1940s view of the east side of Virginia Street, a number of Reno's important, and famous, gambling houses can be seen. At the end of the street is the Riverside Hotel; to its left is a tall construction tower. The Mapes Hotel is under construction and will ultimately change the hotel and casino industry. In 1945, the Nevada legislature imposed stricter controls on gaming licenses and levied a one percent tax on gross earnings. In 1947, the tax was raised to two percent. By the 1940s, gaming was a major economic force in Nevada. (WA-3572; WA-Reno, North Virginia Street.)

Seven
INSTITUTIONS
SCHOOLS, HOSPITALS, AND THE HISTORICAL SOCIETY

Education was important to the people of western towns. Often a school was built before there were any students. Reno's first school was built in 1869—one year after the town was formed. Prof. Orvis Ring stands with his junior high school students in May 1888. Orvis Ring became a school principal and the state superintendent of schools. (ED-325.)

The Nevada Historical Society (NHS) was created in 1904. Newspaper publisher Robert Fulton became president and Jeanne Elizabeth Wier served as executive secretary. Wier, shown at left, would become chairman of the Department of History and Political Science at the University of Nevada and director of the NHS until her death in 1950. Wier was the driving force behind the organization and collected materials of importance to Nevada's history—newspapers, manuscripts, photographs, maps, books, and artifacts. Wier kept the collections in her home on University Avenue (now Center Street) until the NHS had a permanent facility in 1913. (BIO-W-156.)

The mission of the NHS was to collect, preserve, and interpret the heritage of Nevada, the Great Basin, and the West. The collections formed the core of the NHS's research library and museum exhibits. The first museum and library was on North University Avenue (now Center Street) from 1913 to 1927. (NHS-11.)

The State of Nevada participated in the Transcontinental Highways Exposition by commissioning the State Building in downtown Reno. The initial plan was that the Nevada Historical Society (NHS) would occupy the building after the exposition. As it turned out, the Washoe County Library occupied the main floors in 1930 and the NHS was given the basement. The State Building was the NHS's official home from 1927 to 1965. (WA-1396.)

In 1968, after the State Building was torn down (and the NHS was in storage), a new NHS building, designed by Raymond Hellman, was constructed on the University of Nevada campus. In 1982, a 10,000-square-foot collections storage building with environmentally controlled space was added. The Shepperson Gallery was created with a 1997 capital improvement fund, which allowed better museum and research library space. The Nevada Historical Society is the oldest cultural institution in the state. (NHS-482.)

In 1862, Washoe Clinic was founded to treat victims of a smallpox outbreak, and in 1864, the first hospital building was purchased. In 1875, the Washoe County Commissioners purchased 40 acres on the south side of the Truckee River, a mile east of Reno, for a poor farm. A county hospital opened on the site on Mill Avenue in April 1876. Washoe County Hospital (above) was built in 1904 and replaced in 1932. Renown Hospital now occupies the site. (WA-1420.)

In 1897, the Dominican Sisters built a convent school (above, right) on Sixth Street near Chestnut Street (later Arlington Avenue). In 1907, they converted the school to Sisters' Hospital, with just two nurses. In 1912, they built a new Sisters' Hospital (above, left) beside the first hospital, and the two buildings became St. Mary's Hospital. From 1908 until 1923, the hospital operated a training school for nurses. (WA-1423.)

The Nevada State Asylum (above) and a house for the resident physician were built in 1882. Prior to that, Nevada's mentally ill were housed in California hospitals. In *Annie's Ghost*, Steve Luxemberg says, "Working with the insane in the 19th century meant working in an asylum. No specialty known as psychiatry existed. The early psychiatrists were known as *alienists*, reflecting the view that mental illness was outside our understanding." The Stone House was built in 1890 from the remains of a massive 26-foot-high, three-sided wall, built on the site in the mid-1870s to hold a state prison, but never completed. These structures and others were part of a large campus near present-day Galletti Way at Glendale Avenue. Dr. Bergstein, director of the asylum from 1895 through 1898, stands atop the steps of the asylum with his staff. (WA-1402, c. 1900s; WA-1399.)

Central School on West Street, between Fourth and Fifth Streets, was built in 1878. The elementary grades were on the lower floor and the high school was on the upper floor. In 1895, an addition was made on the right of the building and the school became known as Reno High School (above). The school boasted improvements such as steam heat and indoor plumbing. (Reno High 1895, Neal Cobb Collection.)

Reno superintendent of schools B. D. Billinghurst negotiated the construction of the first two of the "four sisters" elementary schools, each with a single tower, built between 1910 and 1912 for $100,000. McKinley Park School on Riverside Drive and Orvis Ring School (above) by East Seventh Street and Evans Avenue were built in the California mission style, designed by architect George A. Ferris. (ED-222.)

The next two of the "Spanish Quartet," Mary S. Doten School on Fifth Street and Mount Rose School (above) on Lander Street, each with double towers, and a new Reno High School were built for $250,000. McKinley survives today as McKinley Arts and Culture Center, and Mount Rose School still operates as an elementary school with the strong support of its neighbors. (ED-214.)

In 1911, a new Reno High School was built on the site of the earlier high school, which was dismantled, piece by piece, for reuse elsewhere. The architecture of this new high school, also designed by George A. Ferris, closely resembled that of the Spanish Quartet. In 1951, Reno High moved to its current location on Booth and Foster Streets and the older high school became Central Junior High. After an explosion and fire, it was torn down in 1968. (Reno High 1911, Neal Cobb Collection.)

In 1874, the Land Grant University of Nevada opened in Elko. In 1886, the university was moved to Reno. Morrill Hall (above) was built in 1886 and, for 10 years, housed the administration offices, classrooms, and dormitory. The building was entered in the National Register of Historic Places in 1974. In 1896, Manzanita Hall (below), the first women's dormitory, was built. A men's dormitory, Lincoln Hall, was also built in 1896. (ED-539; ED-606.)

The years 1894 to 1914 were a period of great progress for the university. In 1907, Clarence Mackay and his mother, Marie Louise Mackay, gave the university the Mackay School of Mines building in honor of his father and her husband, John Mackay, a Comstock "Silver King." A statue of John Mackay was created by Gutzon Borglum of Mount Rushmore fame. The building and the statue were dedicated in 1908 (below). Clarence Mackay served on the building committees of the university from 1907 until his death in 1938. During those years, the Mackay family bequeathed more than $1.5 million for the mining school's endowment, the quad, an athletic field, land acquisitions, and Mackay Science Hall. (WA-549; ED-544.)

The Gates of Opportunity were donated to the university by the class of 1899. The iron gates, seen in this view, are attached to stone pillars at the Ninth Street entrance to the campus. By 1921, the entrance road needed to be widened to accommodate automobiles. The gates were removed, later saved from a scrap metal pile, and now front a home on University Terrace. (ED-734.)

The University of Nevada's first football team sits for a photograph in 1899. Initially the team was unofficially known as the "Sagebrushers" after Nevada's state flowering plant, the sagebrush. In 1923, the students officially designated "Wolves" as the school's mascot and, in 1929, the name Wolf Pack was adopted. (ED-818.)

The quadrangle at the University of Nevada was modeled on Thomas Jefferson's design of the University of Virginia lawn. In this 1944 aerial view of the campus, the tree-lined quad is seen on the right with Mackay School of Mines at the far end, and Morrill Hall (1886) in the foreground. The original names of the buildings are listed with the date they were built in parentheses: men's dormitory, Lincoln Hall (1896); women's dormitory, Manzanita (1896); Mackay School of Mines (1908); first library (1914), now Jones Visitor's Center; Veterinary Building (1914) now gone; Agriculture (1918), now Frandsen Humanities; Education (1920), now Thompson Student Services; Federal Mining Experimental Station (1921), now Facilities Management; Memorial Library, the second library (1927), now Clark Administration; Mackay Science Hall (1930); and Palmer Engineering (1941). These buildings, with Morrill Hall, and two landscape features, the university quadrangle (1908) and Manzanita Lake (1911), form the University of Nevada Historic District, which was placed in the National Register of Historic Places on February 25, 1987. Mackay Stadium is the north edge of the campus in 1944. (ED-673.)

Young thespians at the University of Nevada perform the play *East Lynn* in 1893. (ED-339.)

During the Great Depression, the Works Progress Administration (WPA) provided jobs for people by creating public programs. Workers built roads, bridges, schools, hospitals, and other structures that served the needs of the citizens. The workers are building the Ninth Street retaining wall at the University of Nevada as a WPA project. Virginia Lake in south Reno was also built by the WPA. (MSNC278.)

Eight
ORGANIZATIONS
SOCIAL, FRATERNAL, AND RELIGIOUS

In describing the development of frontier towns, historian Russell Elliott, in his 1973 *History of Nevada*, wrote, "Generally after the first newspapers came the schools, the churches, and the fraternal organizations." Reno had a newspaper in July 1868, a school and the first fraternal organization in 1869, and the first church building in 1870. The Pythian Sisterhood, an auxiliary to the Knights of Pythias Reno Amity Lodge, wore full regalia in this 1910 photograph. (WA-3406.)

In his 1913 book, *History of Nevada*, Sam Davis devoted an entire chapter to fraternal orders, which were important organizations on the mining frontier. Groups like the Knights of Pythias (above), the Masons, and the Odd Fellows (IOOF) offered a social outlet, but also social benefits, such as insurance policies and death benefits for members, and aid to the poor, the widowed, and the orphaned. Reno Masonic Lodge No. 13 was organized in 1869. Meetings were held in the Odd Fellows Hall, the Oasis Saloon, and Alhambra Hall. In 1872, the Masons constructed their own building on Commercial Row and Sierra Street, with a hardware store on the first floor. Reno photographer F. P. Dann, who arrived in Reno in 1896, captured the Masonic group in fraternal regalia, possibly laying a cornerstone or lifting a stone monument (below). (WA-9531; WA-8190.)

During the Tonopah-Goldfield mining boom, a number of fraternal organizations were formed in Nevada, including the Benevolent and Protective Order of Elks, the Fraternal Order of Eagles, the Knights of Columbus, and the United Ancient Order of Druids. The latter formed in Reno in 1901. The Reno Fraternal Order of Eagles Aerie No. 207 was the first to organize in Nevada. The Odd Fellows (above) pose in full regalia. The Shriners organized the Kerak Temple in Reno on December 10, 1906; they march in a 1920 parade in full regalia (below). (NHS-IOOF; WA-Reno, Shriners.)

The Reno Lodge No. 597 of the Benevolent and Protective Order of Elks was organized in 1900. The national organization was founded in 1868 to "promote, protect and enhance the welfare and happiness of each other." One of the benefits of the society was a home to its elderly members. The Elk's Home on First and Sierra Streets was built in 1904. Below, the Elks pose in front of the Elk's Home on Parade Day in 1915. The building was seriously damaged in a 1957 downtown explosion and was demolished soon afterwards. (WA-3344, 1920s; WA-8043.)

The Twentieth Century Club was organized in 1894, and its charter was for the broader culture and the promotion of public welfare. The club started a circulation library in 1894 and founded the first kindergarten in 1901. The Twentieth Century Club building, on West First Street, was constructed in 1925. They offered the building for weddings, luncheons, bridge parties, and dances. The building was sold in 1980, but the club still exists as a Reno institution. Anne Martin, once a University of Nevada professor, was an organizer of the women's suffrage movement and a member of the Twentieth Century Club. She ran twice, unsuccessfully, for the U.S. Senate. (Curtis-134; BIO-M-56.)

By 1879, five denominations had built churches in downtown Reno. The first to build were the Methodists, who dedicated their church at First and Sierra Streets in 1870. The congregation soon outgrew the small building, and in 1900 a new church was built on the site. In 1925, the large congregation dedicated the church (above) at First and West Streets, which still stands on the north side of the Truckee River today. (WA-2805.)

The Great Fire of 1879 struck Reno and its only Catholic church. A new church, St. Mary's, was destroyed by fire in 1905. On June 21, 1908, a new Catholic church, St. Thomas Aquinas, was dedicated at Second and Chestnut Streets (now Arlington Avenue), but was destroyed by fire on December 21, 1909. In 1910, the church was rebuilt (at left) and recently celebrated its 100th anniversary. (WA-9757.)

In 1918, Reno's Congregational church (founded in 1871) and the First Presbyterian Church of Reno (founded in 1902) adopted a temporary wartime federation to support a church building and a pastor. They used the 1892 Congregational church at Fifth and Virginia Streets. The union, known as the Federated Congregational Presbyterian Church, lasted until 1970. (WA-5358.)

In 1876, the Baptists built a church on Second Street between Virginia and Sierra Streets, only to have it burn in the Great Fire of 1879. In 1880, they built a second church on the same site. In 1889, that church was also destroyed by fire. The congregation built a church at West Second and Arlington Streets in 1890 (at left). (WA-2787.)

Reno's Jewish community was held together by its B'nai B'rith Lodge and, in 1871, it purchased property for a cemetery. In 1914, the group formed Congregation Emanu-El and held services in local meeting halls. In 1921, the first services were held in Temple Emanu-El, at 426 West Street. Torn down in 1970, the location is now the site of the Silver Legacy parking garage. (WA-4328.)

In 1938, Luella Garvey, a wealthy widow from Southern California, donated funds to the First Church of Christ, Scientist, for a new building. Garvey recommended the noted African American architect Paul Revere Williams, who had designed her home on California Avenue. He created a distinctive neoclassical revival church near the Truckee River. The church was completed in 1939 and held services until 1998. It is currently being restored and remodeled as a theater. (WA-First Church.)

Nine
COMING OF AGE
PEOPLE, OCCUPATIONS, AND BUSINESSES

C. W. Brooks started Model Dairy in 1906. In 1914, he introduced the first motorized milk delivery in Nevada, replacing horse-drawn wagons. In 1930, the operator of the Model Dairy bottling machine set up the bottles and controlled the flow of milk. Model Dairy has been making dairy products for northern Nevada for more than 100 years. (WA-485.)

In 1895, Reno's Sunset Telephone and Telegraph completed the first municipal telephone system in Nevada. In 1906, the company became Pacific Telephone and Telegraph, and later Nevada Bell. By 1920, telephone lines crisscrossed the state. In 1930, dial telephones began to replace earlier instruments, and by the 1950s, modern switchboards were installed in Reno. (WA-1714.)

In 1908, staff and customers stand outside the People's Store at Second and Virginia Streets. The store offered all manner of clothing for the well-dressed gentleman, including suspenders, hats, suits with vests, ties, and double-breasted suits. (WA-1817.)

George Nixon came to Nevada in 1881 as a bank cashier, became a Winnemucca banker, and in 1891, became a member of the Nevada Assembly. He partnered with George Wingfield in mining investments in Goldfield. They controlled Goldfield Consolidated Mine Company, the richest mining property in Nevada. Nixon, a Republican, was elected in 1905 to the U.S. Senate, reelected in 1911, and served until his death in 1912. (BIO-N-22.)

Francis Newlands came to Nevada in 1888 to manage the affairs of Comstock silver baron William Sharon. Newlands was elected to the U.S. House of Representatives in 1892 and to the U.S. Senate in 1903. He died in office in 1917. Senator Newlands was the primary author of the Reclamation Act of 1902, known as the Newlands Irrigation Project, which brought water from the Truckee River to the Lahontan Valley, creating the farming communities of Fernley and Fallon. (BIO-N-98.)

The architectural career of Reno native Frederic DeLongchamps spanned the years 1907 to 1965. He designed nine courthouses and more than 500 other buildings. In downtown Reno, his commissions include the Riverside, the post office, and the Washoe Courthouse. His work dominates downtown Carson City, including Heroes Memorial Building, the first Nevada Supreme Courthouse, and Ormsby County Courthouse. He designed older parts of the University of Nevada campus. (BIO-D-211.)

When the railroad was the most common means of traveling across the United States, politicians chartered tour trains to go from town to town. On a whistle-stop campaign trip, a candidate would give a speech from the rear platform of the train, but rarely set foot on the ground. Franklin Roosevelt was one of the last presidents to regularly use this means of campaigning. On the back of the train, in 1939, are Pres. Franklin Roosevelt and Nevada's U.S. senators Pat McCarran and Key Pittman. (BIO-R-336.)

Samuel Clemens, the revered author known as Mark Twain, began his literary career in Nevada. He came to Nevada in 1861 with his brother Orion, the secretary of the Nevada Territory, appointed by Pres. Abraham Lincoln. In 1862, Clemens tried mining in Aurora, living in a dirt-floor cabin (below) with other miners. Clemens wrote for the *Virginia City Territorial Enterprise*, covering the Nevada legislature. Pictured at right are, from left to right, Nevada House member A. J. Simmons, Samuel Clemens (aka Mark Twain), and Nevada House member Wm. H. Claggett. While at the *Territorial Enterprise*, Clemens took the pen name Mark Twain, and was known for his joking and humorous style and for mixing fact with fantasy in his reporting. When his teasing, in print, brought him three concurrent duel challenges, he left hurriedly in May 1864. (BIO-T-131; MIN-4328.)

As early as 1874, Reno had a vigilante group, the "601," that took care of crime. A fire police unit was appointed in 1877. A town deputy took care of problems until the City of Reno was incorporated in 1903 and a chief of police was appointed. A jail facility was provided in city hall in August 1906. A. A. Burke (above, center front) was the second police chief in Reno, serving from 1907 to 1911. Officers walked downtown beats and had call boxes for communication. In the 1920s, Reno officers (below), from left to right, Harry Fletcher, Bill Dean, and Dick Heap rode motorcycles as part of police duty. By the 1930s, the police had squad cars. The first radio communication began in 1934. (WA-1459; WA-1462.)

Entering a drugstore (above) in the early 1900s, customers saw merchandise behind counters, out of reach, and had to ask the clerk for items of interest. The pharmacist was at the back of the drugstore ready to prepare prescriptions and give advice. The soda fountain and the tables and chairs were for enjoying wonderful concoctions, like sodas, malts, milk shakes, or sundaes. In a print shop (below), the compositor set type and a pressman worked the press, a labor-intensive activity. The process was offset printing, an 1870 technology where inked images were transferred from a plate, to a rubber blanket, and then to paper. Most Reno city lots were 25 feet wide and 125 feet deep, hence the long, narrow workspace. (Curtis-205; WA-1908.)

The hardwood floors at the Wedekind Grocery Store (above) were washed nightly. Most items were behind the counter and retrieved by the clerk who wrote the items on an invoice and totaled the sale in his head. There were not many fresh items— mostly canned goods, candy, and baking materials. The customer could charge the purchase and pay at the end of the month. The Reno Meat Company (below) had meat hanging on racks and butchers available to cut pieces. Purchases were also tallied by hand. Both stores offered home delivery. (WA-5649; WA-5648.)

During World War II, Pacific Amusements, run by Jerry Cobb, provided a jukebox-like setup for bars, restaurants, and social establishments. Put a nickel in a Wurlitzer-like device, tell the operator what song you would like, and presto, there was music. The system was commonly known as Telephono and had 3,000 records to choose from, making it a better deal than the jukebox. Operators (below), located in the Byington Building on Second Street between Virginia and Sierra Streets, would select a record, put it on a turntable, and music would be distributed using the phone system. (Neal Cobb Collection.)

In 1908, the men of the Washoe County Sheriff's Department pose on the steps of the office. Sheriff C. P. Ferrell stands in the center. In 1912, dentist Henry O'Neill (below) is ready to work on a patient. Dental offices began using electricity after 1900. Novacaine was introduced in 1907. Penicillin was invented in 1929 and later applied as an antibiotic for dental infections. In 1939, dentures sent by mail were declared unlawful in the United States. (WA-1363; WA-1706.)

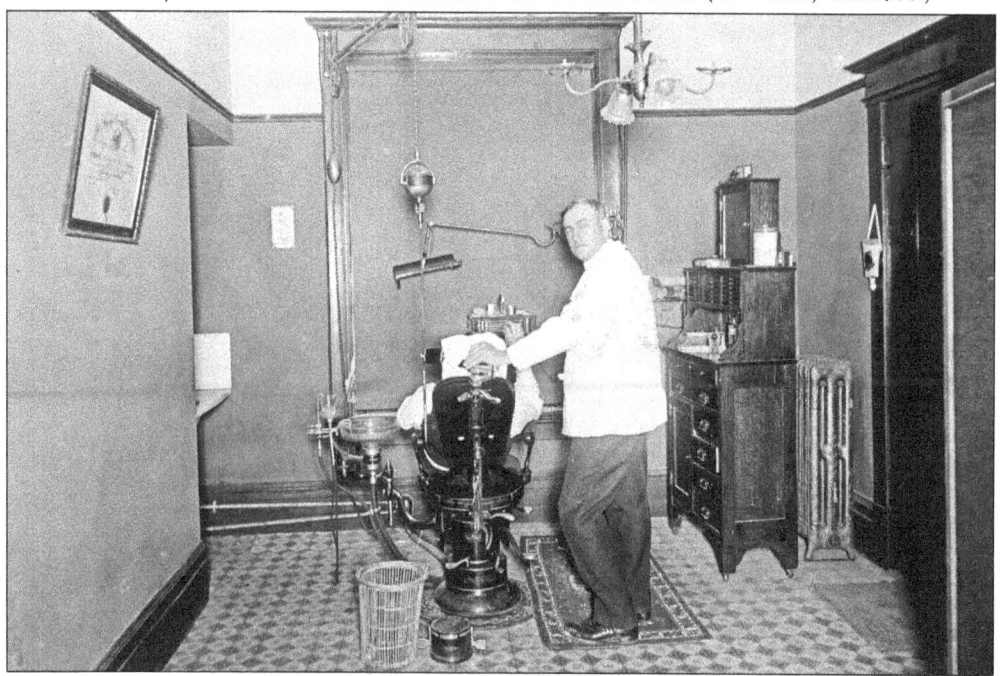

Ten
How Reno Plays
Entertainment and Recreation

Baseball started in the mid-1800s in the United States. By the 1860s, there were professional and semiprofessional leagues. Reno had baseball at Moana Stadium by 1905 and Threkel Park, off Fourth Street, in the 1930s and 1940s. Reno had a semiprofessional league, the Silver Sox, in the 1940s. City leagues probably began in the 1890s, and Little League began in 1939. An 1890s Reno baseball team, the Overland Team, looked into the camera. (WA-3445.)

Around 1900, a Reno Wheelmen bicycle team poses for a picture (above). The Reno Wheelmen Club was founded in 1896. As the 19th century gave way to the 20th, the club boasted more than 400 members, at a time when Reno's population was only about 4,000. The bicycle was important for transportation and recreation. The Reno Wheelmen had their own clubhouse, called Wheelman Hall, with a weight room, swimming pool, and a social hall where they held concerts, dances, and plays. They even had their own band and football team. Club member and racer George Kommayer is assisted by trainer King Ryan at left. (WA-3381; WA-3368.)

Moana Springs opened as a resort in October 1905, with a large bathhouse, a pool fed by hot springs, a stately hotel, clubhouse, baseball diamond, and picnic grounds. It was served by the Nevada Interurban Trolley line from 1907 to 1920. Moana Springs hosted dances, rodeos, boxing matches, trap shoots, circuses, and aviation exhibitions. The City of Reno purchased Moana Springs in 1956 to build a new recreational complex. (WA-1950.)

April 3, 1911, was Roosevelt Day in Reno. Former president Teddy Roosevelt gave a dramatic speech at the University of Nevada. Crowds gathered at the university and followed the presidential vehicle along the parade route. (BIO-R-195.)

Live theater and movies have had a long history in Reno. In 1887, Jacob McKissick built the McKissick Opera House and Hotel on the corner of Plaza and Sierra Streets. A local troupe gave the opening performance of *Ramona*. For more than 30 years, the McKissick remained the premiere Reno entertainment venue. The railroads offered special stopover privileges to New York theater companies en route to San Francisco. (WA-1612; WA-3518.)

The Grand Theater (above) opened in 1904 as a vaudeville house, and as motion pictures came into vogue, expanded to include three small movie theaters. In 1908, the Wigwam (below) opened on Second Street near Sierra Street, featuring both live acts and movies for an admission fee of 10¢. The theater was remodeled in 1942 and became the Nevada Theater. Remodeled completely in 1948, it was renamed the Crest and entertained audiences until 1977. From 1934, the Wigwam Coffee Shop, on the left of the building, sold its famous hot apple pie. Reno Little Theater held performances on North Sierra Street from 1941 to 1996, the location now a Circus Circus parking garage. Founded in 1935 and soon to open its own theater again, it is the oldest continually operating performing arts theater in Nevada. (WA-3516; WA-1738.)

In 1910, Jim Jeffries, the former undefeated heavyweight champion, came out of retirement to fight the black heavyweight champion Jack Johnson. Jeffries stated, "I feel obligated to the sporting public at least to make an effort to reclaim the heavyweight championship for the white race . . . I should step into the ring again and demonstrate that a white man is king of them all." Jeffries had not fought in six years and had to lose weight to get back to his championship fighting weight. The trains and huge crowds arrived at the Reno Depot. Reno had a population of 10,000 at the time. Fifteen special trains brought enough people to swell the fight crowd to 23,000. (WA-Johnson-Jeffries fight poster; WA-7991.)

After California banned the match in San Francisco, the "Fight of the Century" was moved to Reno, to be held on July 4, 1910. Reno was always looking for a way to promote itself and boxing filled the bill. Practice sessions were staged at the Johnson training camp in July 1910 (above). The Johnson-Jeffries fight took place at the southwest corner of Fourth and Toano Streets in Reno, where a marker memorializes the event. In the fight, Johnson won the match in the 15th round. The referee called the fight before the 10-second count was given and raised Johnson's arm. The fight was refereed by legendary fight promoter Tex Rickard, who brought the fight to Reno. Many other fights have been fought in Nevada, but this was one of the most famous. (WA-3671; MS-Cussick-JJ-2.)

Coney Island's elaborate amusement park opened to the public on June 20, 1909. The founder, Otto G. Benschuetz, landscaped the grounds, put in a children's playground, a bandstand for outdoor concerts, and a dance pavilion that also served as a skating rink and theatre. Coney Island had an artificial lake filled with water from the Truckee River, complete with boats, covered landings and bathhouses. The park enjoyed good access from a trolley system that ran along the road that connected Reno with Sparks. A special weekend trolley fare was 5¢ to and from the popular site. The park closed after Benschuetz's death in 1912, and the site was turned into the Coney Island Auto Camp. (WA-1015; WA-1014.)

Coney Island offered free admission on Sunday, June 27, 1909. (WA-Coney Island ad.)

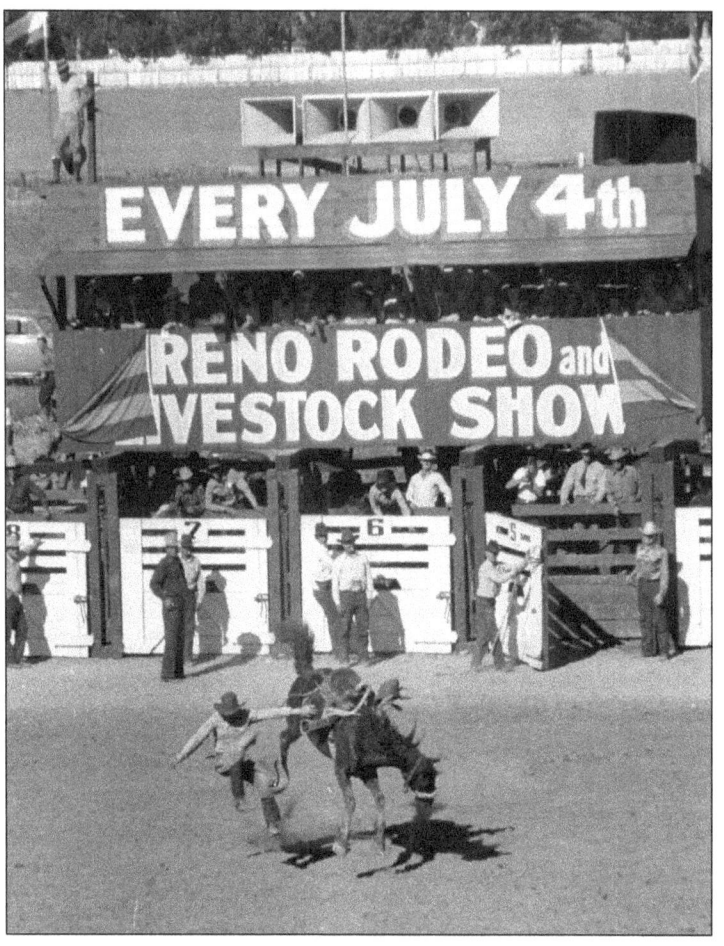

The Reno Rodeo, a weeklong event, has been held at the Washoe County Fairgrounds since 1919. Cowboys who compete in today's rodeo follow the rugged tradition of their 18th- and 19th-century predecessors. To succeed in the early West, cowboys had to develop roping and riding skills. Contests to determine who could rope a calf quickest or ride the wildest horse were common practice. Roping and riding events were often staged in a convenient corral or pasture. Today's cowboys, members of the Professional Rodeo Cowboy Association, compete for prizes at as many as 600 rodeos around the country. (WA-3463; WA-Reno Rodeo, 1932.)

Ernie Mack photographed the Reno Rodeo Parade in 1939. Rodeo flags welcoming each state flew above Reno streets to welcome people from all 48 states coming to attend the biggest and richest rodeo in the world. A rodeo queen, selected every year since 1920, was crowned as goodwill ambassador of the Reno Rodeo. Each year, volunteer cowboys and cowgirls run a four-day, 60-mile cattle drive, bringing a herd of 300 cattle from the Rancho Haven area to the Reno Rodeo grounds. The Southern Pacific Depot illustration (below) by Lew Hymers promoted Reno as a rodeo town. (WA-Reno Rodeo Parade; WA-SPRR Depot.)

Parades of all kinds were popular with Reno residents. In 1917, Reno's Loyalty Day parade honored those fighting for freedom in the Great War (later known as World War I). Participants carrying flags crossed the Virginia Street Bridge and walked or drove north on Virginia Street. The YMCA building is on the right. (WA-5280.)

Recognize these cowboy actors under the Reno arch? The movie *Virginia City*, starring Errol Flynn, Randolph Scott, Miriam Hopkins, and Humphrey Bogart, premiered in Virginia City and Reno in 1940, although none of the actual filming was done in Virginia City. All actors in the movie and anyone under contract to Warner Brothers were required to attend every world premiere; therefore, many actors around town and in the photograph were not in the movie. Ronald Reagan is second from left; in the center are Errol Flynn on the dark horse and William Boyd (Hopalong Cassidy) on the white. (WA-7420.)

BIBLIOGRAPHY

activetectonics.la.asu.edu/kites/06eq.html
Angel, Myron. *Thompson and West History of Nevada*. Oakland, CA: Pacific Press, Printers, Stereotypers, and Binders, 1881, reprinted 1958.
Barber, Alicia. *Reno's Big Gamble: Image and Reputation in the Biggest Little City*. Lawrence, KS: University Press of Kansas, 2008.
Cafferata, Patty. *Lake Mansion: Home to Reno's Founding Families*. Reno, NV: Eastern Slope Publishers, 2008.
Central Pacific Railroad Museum. www.cprr.org
Cobb, Neal and Fenwick, Jerry. *Reno, Now and Then*. Reno, NV: University of Nevada Oral History Program, 2008.
Davis, Samuel. *History of Nevada*. Reno, NV: Elms Publishing Company, 1913.
Elliott, Russell R. *History of Nevada*. Lincoln, NB: University of Nebraska Press, 1973.
Historic Reno Preservation Society. *FootPrints*, vols. 7–13.
Hulse, James W. *The Nevada Adventure: A History*. Reno, NV: University of Nevada Press, 1961.
Land, Barbara, and Myrick Land. *A Short History of Reno*, Reno, NV: University of Nevada Press, 1995.
Myrick, David F. *Railroads of Nevada and Eastern California*, vol. 1. Berkeley, CA: Howell-North Books, 1962.
www.nps.gov/history/nr/travel/nevada
Nevada Historical Society Quarterlies. (Volume-Number) 23-1, 26-2, 32-3, 33-1, 35-3, 38-1, 38-3, 40-3, 41-1, 42-1, 43-2, 44-3, 46-2, 47-1, 49-3, 50-1.
www.onlinenevada.org
Paher, Stanley W. *Reno 100 Years Old: Celebrates Birthday*, Gateway Press, Las Vegas, NV, 1968, from *Nevada State Journal*, May 2 and 9, 1968.
Parker, James L., Reno Department of Police. "Our First One Hundred Years." April, 1978.
Rocha, Guy Louis. "Reno's First Robber Baron." *Nevada Magazine*, March/April, 1980.
www.wikipedia.org

Visit us at
arcadiapublishing.com